THE WHISTLEBLOWER

THE WHISTLEBLOWER

SEX TRAFFICKING,
MILITARY CONTRACTORS, AND
ONE WOMAN'S FIGHT FOR JUSTICE

KATHRYN BOLKOVAC

WITH

CARI LYNN

palgrave
macmillan

First published in 2011 by
PALGRAVE MACMILLAN®
in the United States—a division of St. Martin's Press LLC,
175 Fifth Avenue, New York, NY 10010.

Where this book is distributed in the UK, Europe and the rest of the
world, this is by Palgrave Macmillan, a division of Macmillan Publishers
Limited, registered in England, company number 785998, of Houndmills,
Basingstoke, Hampshire RG21 6XS.

Palgrave Macmillan is the global academic imprint of the above companies
and has companies and representatives throughout the world.

Palgrave® and Macmillan® are registered trademarks in the United States,
the United Kingdom, Europe and other countries.

All photos have been provided by Kathryn Bolkovac and are printed with
permission.

ISBN: 978–0–230–10802–8

Library of Congress Cataloging-in-Publication Data

Bolkovac, Kathryn.
    The whistleblower : sex trafficking, military contractors, and one
    woman's fight for justice / Kathryn Bolkovac with Cari Lynn.
        p. cm.
    ISBN 978–0–230–10802–8
        1. Whistle blowing—Bosnia and Hercegovina. 2. Whistle blowing—
    United States. 3. Human trafficking—Bosnia and Hercegovina. 4. Private
    military companies—Bosnia and Hercegovina. 5. Bolkovac, Kathryn.
    I. Lynn, Cari. II. Title.

HD60.5.B54B65 2010
364.15—dc22   2010023196

A catalogue record of the book is available from the British Library.

Design by Newgen Imaging Systems (P) Ltd., Chennai, India.

First edition: January 2011

10 9 8 7 6 5 4 3 2 1

Printed in the United States of America.

CONTENTS

AUTHOR'S NOTE AND ACKNOWLEDGMENTS

This is a true story, my story. In telling it, I collaborated with a co-writer, Cari Lynn, whom I would like to thank. The writing process has included our drawing from an extensive array of official documents, reports, notes, transcripts, tape recordings, witness statements, personal interviews, emails, publications, news articles, BBC documentaries, and the lengthy decision by the tribunal that heard my case in the United Kingdom. Sources of the documents include the United Nations, the U.S. Department of State, the U.S. Department of Justice, DynCorp, Human Rights Watch, local Bosnian police authorities, and various other international organizations. In writing the book, we also relied on numerous books and journal articles on military contractors and human trafficking. Where there was no tape recording or published account of a conversation or situation I was involved in, I have reconstructed the events and dialogue to the best of my recollection. In certain cases, I have changed people's names and identifying characteristics. I have also utilized some composites, wherein I combined common characteristics and circumstances and attributed these to individual characters, especially with regard to trafficking victims.

It is important for me to thank my solicitor, Karen Bailey, and barrister, Stephanie Harrison, of the UK, who skillfully and doggedly waged the battle in my effort to expose the truth. I could not have done this without their advice and support. I would like to thank Ms. Madeleine Rees, for her courage in speaking the truth regarding highly inappropriate actions that were being undertaken by UN officials, DynCorp employees, and other internationals within the mission. She provided insight and information that was invaluable to winning my case. My IPTF colleagues Bo Andreasson and Thor Arnason for their long lasting friendship and humor when light-hearted moments were few.

I am grateful to *The Whistleblower* movie team, especially director/writer Larysa Kondracki and writer Eilis Kirwan, who had the tenacity to show up at my doorstep one day several years ago asking permission to interview me and, along with Christina Piovesan and Amy Kaufman, the perseverance to make a movie. My special thanks to actress Rachel Weisz for her commitment to get this story told.

I must acknowledge the Lincoln Police Department for the support and training that guided me through many trials. International organizations, including the Project on Government Oversight, and Human Rights Watch investigator and attorney Martina Vandenburg, whose due diligence and oversight into government waste, fraud, and abuse is ongoing. My agent Carol Mann and attorney Josh Sandler. Thank you also to Palgrave Macmillan and my editor, Alessandra Bastagli, for giving me the opportunity to tell my story.

Most importantly, thanks to my husband and partner, Jan G. H. van der Velde, my children, Jake Vollertsen, Sarah Kramer, and Erin May, and my parents, Alfred and Sylvia Bolkovac. Their many years of love and patience in understanding this real-life drama was not something they should have had to undertake, but they supported me along every step of the journey.

Map of Bosnia and Herzegovina, 2002. Courtesy of Central Intelligence Agency

PROLOGUE
(April 2001)

"I need to speak with the ambassador."

My palm was sweating as I gripped the receiver. After being transferred around the switchboard, I finally had one of the ambassador's assistants on the line. I was using the phone of a Swedish friend and colleague, Lotta, who for the past few nights had graciously given me her house keys and made up the couch because I had been too rattled to stay at my own place.

"May I ask what this is regarding?" the assistant asked.

"I'm an American. My name is Kathryn Bolkovac. He'll know who I am."

"I'm sorry, but Ambassador Miller is scheduled to be boarding a flight now. May I have him phone you on Monday?"

Monday? No, I was reaching out to the American embassy in Bosnia-Herzegovina because I was in need of assistance—now. "Please," I said, "it's an emergency."

There was a pause on the line, and I was certain she could hear the quivering in my voice. It was my personal source of pride that I had spent my entire police career clear-headed and tough under pressure, but my situation was dire.

"All right," she said, "let me see if I can patch you through to his mobile."

After numerous clicks, there was the sudden rushing sound of wind and propellers. A voice shouted above the noise. "This is Tom Miller."

"Ambassador Miller, this is Kathryn Bolkovac—"

"Sorry, I can't hear you. Can you speak up?"

I raised my voice. "This is Kathryn Bolkovac. As you know, I've been terminated by DynCorp—"

"I'm on a tarmac, could you please speak louder?"

I yelled into the phone, "I've been terminated by DynCorp and was told the State Department pulled my contract and that you were a part of this decision."

Through the noise, he shouted that he was not privy to any such decision.

Was DynCorp once again passing the buck, this time trying to use the U.S. ambassador as its fall guy? But I continued, at the top of my lungs, "I have been threatened by my superiors at DynCorp—"

The roar of the propellers grew even louder. "I'm sorry," he interrupted, "but I can barely hear you at all, and I need to get on a plane. Call my secretary and make an appointment for next week, okay? We'll meet next week, okay? Thank you."

The noise silenced as the phone went dead. My own voice echoed in my ears and in the quiet of the tiny rented house. I must have been absentmindedly pacing, for I was entangled in the old-fashioned, wiry phone cord still commonplace in residences in Sarajevo. I spun myself from the cord, like I used to do as a kid. *You're really on your own now, Bolkovac*, I thought.

All I could do at this point was put everything I owned in my car and get out. I had my most vital belonging with me: a khaki Eddie Bauer duffel bag. The bag had started this journey as an innocent carry-on, packed with a travel pillow and an extra sweater. Now it was filled with incriminating evidence I had collected over the past two years. Evidence that could implicate personnel of one of the most powerful corporations in the world—funded by billions of

U.S. taxpayer dollars—with involvement in one of the most profitable and licentious forms of organized crime.

I locked up Lotta's house and slid the key under the front door, then hurried to my parked car. The previous year, I had used the very attractive discount offered to United Nations employees to buy a royal blue Mercedes in Sarajevo. It was cheaper than a Chevy would be back in the States, and I loved this car. But now it was on my list of things I was wary of. Back when I was a new recruit, a station commander had warned me that car accidents happen in this country all the time—I had rolled my eyes at his air-quoted "accidents," knowing he was prone to drama. Recently, however, my subconscious had dug this conversation back up, and the words replayed in my mind. I locked the duffel bag in the trunk and turned the ignition.

The engine started with its typical hum, and I sank into the seat, momentarily relieved. As much as I did not want to set foot back in my own house, I could not leave without collecting some things, specifically a box of letters from my children. For two years my teenagers hand-wrote letters to me, and I would be damned if I was run out of the country without those. I had made difficult choices as a mother, but thinking about the letters from my children gave me a spark of determination, reminding me how proud the family had been when I started on this mission, how optimistic we were about all the good, meaningful work I was going to do and how much of a difference I could make.

I drove through the city, passing the tall wrought-iron gates of the American embassy, the Stars and Stripes proudly snapping in the breeze. Not long ago, I had lingered at those gates, telling jokes with the Marines standing guard before being welcomed inside to mingle with diplomats and eat ice cream sundaes from a McDonald's tent set up on the terrace. Now, for the first time, I understood what it must be like to be a person without a country. I had used that phrase many times in my human rights work, to describe the young women who had gone through hell and back only to be denied reentrance to their home countries because of ridiculous technicalities and gaping holes in the law. "Original passport confiscated. Denied reissuance. Status: without a country" was a verdict I had written time and time again in my reports before having to hand my paperwork, along with the frightened young women, over to the International Organization for Migration (IOM).

I pulled up in the gravel drive of my accommodations (this was what everyone on the mission called our rentals; no one ever referred to their place as "home"), a quaint farmhouse that I rented from a young Serbian landlady named Branca. She had grown up in this house but, after her father died, Branca had squeezed into the small guesthouse around back along with her entire extended family. The rent we internationals paid was her family's primary income. I occupied the first floor, and an oak staircase led to my roommate's quarters, although he had taken leave back to the United States for health reasons. I had chosen this house for its location on Vrelo Bosne, the Central Park of Sarajevo.

At the source of the river Bosna, the Vrelo (which means "spring" in Serbo-Croatian) had picture-postcard views in every direction, with waterfalls and still pools framed by snow-capped mountains rising up in the hazy distance. On weekends, I would stroll for hours down paths shaded by a canopy of trees, past horse-drawn carriages clip-clopping along, and over footbridges with pebble-covered streams gurgling beneath my feet. You could see people from all walks of life in the park: foreigners who had money would dine at the outdoor cafes, locals would bring a bag from the market to make a picnic in the grass, and the kerchief-wrapped Roma would beg and linger until they were chased away. It was near effortless to lose yourself in the landscape, completely forgetting what part of the world you were in. That is, until you stumbled upon the red-and-white tape and BEWARE signs, reminding you that this peaceful park had been part of the front lines and that the surrounding hills were still riddled with landmines.

As I approached the front door of my accomodations, my stomach churned, and I prepared myself to find the place turned upside down. I pushed open the door.

The place wasn't ransacked. It was cozy and clean, just the way I had left it. I steadied myself. Fear is one thing, but first my car, then the apartment—was I becoming paranoid? Paranoia for a cop is like a tremor for a surgeon.

Ridding the notion from my head, I pulled down my suitcase from the top of the closet and emptied the bureau drawers, including the bundle of letters from my children. I did not have much in the way of clothes to pack since I had worn the International Police Task Force uniform—blue khakis, button-down top—every day. I threw in socks and underwear, my gym clothes, a couple pairs of jeans, some sweatshirts, and the long black dress I had worn once, to the Fourth of July party at the embassy. I already had turned in the rest of my gear: flak jacket; emergency evacuation bag; blue helmet; and leather utility belt, which was basically a holster for a Maglite since we were not authorized to carry a gun on this UN peacekeeping mission.

I took a quick glance around to see if there was anything I had missed. Branca's mother's collections were everywhere—little figurines, carved relics, trinkets—all displayed on hand-crocheted doilies. "Knicky-knacky, ticky-tacky" is how my own mother would have described the style. But in Bosnia these objects were not garage-sale fare; they signified that the family had enough money to acquire possessions. When Branca's mother had learned I was Catholic, she scanned her collection and ceremoniously chose a tiny brass crucifix, pressing it into my palm and saying it was mine to keep. For her, it was a great source of pride to have belongings that were not only decorative but were nice enough to gift.

Although I was not a particularly religious person, I knew my Hail Marys and Our Fathers and had kept the brass crucifix on my nightstand. I slid it into my pocket and zipped shut my suitcase, leaving behind some khaki pants and a pair of black Army boots, knowing Branca's teenage nephew would appreciate them; besides, I much preferred my Rocky Mountain boots from the police force back home.

As I turned to leave, I spotted a patch of royal blue peeking out from under the bed: my beret, the universal symbol of a UN peace-keeping mission. Apparently I had forgotten to turn it in. I plucked it up and slipped it into my bag.

Just then I heard a car pull up on the gravel driveway. Instinctively, I shut off the light. A car door slammed and a heavy-footed clomp-ing of boots approached. A sharp knock hit the front door.

My right hand slid down my hip. For a decade I had carried a gun there, and it was force of habit to reach for it—only to be reminded that I was unarmed. I glanced around, looking for something to use to defend myself. My closest weapon was a half-finished bottle of gin. I gripped the bottle's neck and stole some glances through the lace curtains of the window. I could see a man's broad back in a blue shirt—possibly a UN uniform. He turned, and I made out a familiar profile. The man was my Icelandic colleague and friend, Thor.

I hurried to the door. "I'm so glad—" I began.

Thor raised an index finger to his lips. Silence. His jaw was clenched and his eyes were steely. I had never seen him look this intense, which was saying a lot for a normally serious Viking. He stepped in and, seeing my suitcase, grabbed it and motioned for me to follow him. I tucked the bottle of gin under my arm, suspecting it might still come in handy.

Thor's white truck, a Land Rover with black UN letters on each side, was in the driveway, and two of his British colleagues from the

Organized Crime Unit, who were also his roommates, were waiting in the backseat. I knew the men, Ian and Bob, from many Saturday nights sitting around in someone's living room with several bottles of wine and a couple of guitars. But now they had their military faces on too, both dead serious.

"Get in," Thor said.

"My car—" I protested, thinking of my duffel bag.

"We need to talk," Thor said firmly. "In my car."

I looked to Ian and Bob, then back to Thor. I had not been staying at my place—how had they known to find me here at this moment? My head said it was okay to trust them, but my feet stayed planted.

Of the three, I knew Thor best; we had become fast friends after traveling together to Hungary for the International Law Enforcement Academy conference. In Budapest, we had had the idea to take a city bus around to sightsee, which was going fine until the bus came to a halt and the lights went off, and we realized we had missed the last stop and were back at the bus barn. The driver refused to take us anywhere else, so after a good laugh we had to hoof it back to the hotel. Then there was the time Thor and I were in the market and I realized I had left my wallet at a vendor's stand. Without a second's hesitation, Thor bolted like an Olympic sprinter through the crowd to rescue my wallet—and he did.

"Kathy," Thor said, jolting me from my thousand-yard stare. "Are you okay?"

Barely. I was near mental and physical exhaustion. My fingertips brushed against the outline of the crucifix in my pocket, and I made a quick promise that when I made it out of Bosnia I would go straight to the confessional. Deciding that I needed to trust these men, I slid into the passenger seat of Thor's car.

"We overheard some chatter at Main HQ," Thor began. "Kathy, we think your phone has been bugged and likely your apartment too. We have reason to believe you're in danger."

Oddly, the first emotion that came to me was relief: I was not alone in sensing possible danger. My mind quickly defaulted to my kids—all the phone conversations we had had; could they be in danger too? Good thing I had kept my maiden name; my children would be much harder to trace with a different last name. Besides, all three lived in different cities, with two in college and the youngest at home with her dad. Thor's voice filtered into my thoughts, and I forced myself to focus. "I know you're planning to leave the country soon," he said, "but you need to stay with us in the meantime, for safety."

"I was going to leave straight from here," I said.

Ian spoke up from the backseat. "You of all people know what goes on after dark on those desolate roads, and that's your only way out. We can't let you leave until sunrise."

I turned to look at them squarely. "What exactly did you hear?"

The three men glanced at each other as if trying to determine how much they could, or should, reveal. Finally Thor said, "Significant chatter, implying bodily harm."

We decided I would stay at their house for the night and leave first thing in the morning. Bob and I got in my car and followed Thor's UN truck to their villa on the northern edge of the city. When we arrived, Thor jumped out, hoisted open a wooden garage door, and motioned me in. We unloaded my bags and then I stepped back to watch as Ian sprinkled a thick coat of baby powder over the ground all around my car.

I spent the night staring at the ceiling, thinking back on the events of my past two years with DynCorp, a billion-dollar Goliath. As a police officer certified in forensic science, I was contracted to work on human rights abuses. When I was promoted to UN Headquarters to oversee all cases of domestic abuse, sexual assault, and human trafficking throughout Bosnia, my case files started disappearing on a routine basis from the Internal Affairs office. Files upon files of evidence we human rights officers, and even local Bosnian police, had collected never saw the light of day: victim statements, license plate numbers, identifying badges, names, tattoos, and even instant photographs. All of it gone. Except, of course, for the copies I had in my Eddie Bauer duffel bag.

I thought of Lotta, who was in her early thirties. She was in Bosnia as a member of the Swedish police force and was simultaneously finishing her master's thesis. We had bonded after she lodged a formal complaint against an American DynCorp contractor who would show up at Main HQ flaunting a suspiciously young foreign girl on his arm. No investigation into whether the girl was a minor—let alone a trafficking victim—was ever initiated, and the only thing to result from Lotta's complaint was that she and I became friends. I hated to think I may have put Lotta in danger, but she was a very smart, capable woman, with a lot of access and know-how. Besides, her mission time was nearly up, and she was almost as anxious to get out as I was.

Sunlight could not come fast enough, and finally the house began to stir. Ian made me a thermos of coffee and packed up some food, while Thor checked the garage for footprints in the powder.

When he gave the go-ahead, I started up my car. He trailed me several miles outside of Sarajevo to make sure I was not being followed, then waved me on. On that day in April 2001, I drove non-stop out of the country. I may have been forced out, but this was not over. DynCorp, global leader in the business of military strategy, nation rebuilding, world security, and counterintelligence, had underestimated one thing: a forty-year-old, divorced mom from Lincoln, Nebraska.

1

RUNNING FROM SOMETHING
(November 1998–June 1999)

T he war in Bosnia was the longest and bloodiest waged on European soil since World War II. In 1992, in the wake of the perfect storm of the fall of communism in Yugoslavia and the increasing power of Serbian president Slobodan Milošević, Bosnia and Herzegovina declared independence from Yugoslavia. A multiethnic region, Bosnia and Herzegovina had long been home to Catholic Croats, Orthodox Serbs, and Muslim Bosniaks. I have Croation roots, and I remember as a teenager spending summer vacations in Ohio with my grandparents, gathering on the front porch while Grandma cross-stitched pillowcases and Grandpa talked about the old country, Croatia, describing the different religions and ethnicities living and working side by side and even intermarrying.

All that changed in April 1992, when Serb forces shelled Sarajevo, targeting Muslims and Croats, looting, burning, and massacring Bosniak-populated regions around the country, including mass attacks at marketplaces and a football stadium. Concentration camps detaining Muslims and Croats were set up in four regions. There, men, women, and children were starved, tortured, and killed. The Serbs would soon establish a complete blockade of Sarajevo, in a siege that would last until 1996 and would go down as the longest siege of a capital city in modern history. During these years, snipers perched in the surrounding hills or on the top floors of the tallest buildings and pecked off approximately 10,000 innocent civilians, including 1,500 children. In the final year of the siege, electricity, water, and food delivery was cut off. In August 1995, NATO—the North Atlantic Treaty Organization—launched air strikes against the Serbs. Facing combined uprisings by Croat and Bosniak forces, the Serbs finally retreated.

The signing of the Dayton Peace Agreement in December 1995 ended the three-and-a-half-year war in the Republic of Yugoslavia, and the region was renamed Bosnia and Herzegovina. In all, approximately 100,000 people, including thousands of children, had been killed; the majority were Muslim Bosniaks. Nearly 2 million people were estimated to have been displaced. Milošević was charged with genocide and crimes against humanity. His trial stretched on for five years until, on March 11, 2006, he was found dead in his prison cell at The Hague, ostensibly from a heart attack, although conspiracy theories abound.

As part of the Dayton agreement, the UN Security Council mandated the creation of a mission in Bosnia and Herzegovina to provide an International Police Task Force (IPTF) and a UN Civilian Affairs Office. Together, the branches had the not-small tasks of: humanitarian relief and refugee aid, de-mining, monitoring human rights issues, facilitating elections, rebuilding infrastructure, rebuilding the economy, and providing civilian police to train and monitor what was left of the diminished local police force.

To make up the IPTF, each UN member state was asked to supply officers from its national police forces. Out shipped officers from the Italian Carabinieri Corps, the German Bundespolizei, the French

Gendarmerie National, the Spanish Guardia Civil, the Canadian Royal Mounted Police, the Dutch Koninklijke Marechaussee, and so on. Because the United States does not have this type of national police force—U.S. police is primarily made up of state, county, and city forces—the American police contingent was to be comprised solely of private contractors.

This mission in Bosnia was a lucrative bid for American private military contractors. The first ever contract of this sort—called a global Logistics Civilian Augmentation Program (Logcap) contract—was won by Houston-based Brown & Root Services. For three years, Brown & Root provided American police to Bosnia and seven other countries. But in 1995 the contract was put back up for competitive bidding, and DynCorp, with headquarters in Virginia, snagged its first global Logcap contract by underbidding the incumbent.

The U.S. State Department cut the checks for DynCorp, and the media was blitzed with press releases. DynCorp would be in charge of everything from placing specialized aircraft mechanics on military bases, to staffing the mess hall cafeteria, to managing warehouses, to engineering new building construction, to recruiting hundreds of American police officers to serve as peacekeepers.

———

I got involved in DynCorp's first rent-a-cop contract simply by answering an ad. It was stapled to the bulletin board at police headquarters in Lincoln, Nebraska, in the autumn of 1998:

International Police Task Force—Bosnia

It caught my eye primarily because the salary figure was twice as high as any I had ever seen posted on a police station bulletin board:

$85,000 a year. A DynCorp logo decorated the top of the ad. I had never heard of DynCorp, so I read further:

> The US State Department is seeking active/retired police officers of any rank who are eager to accept a challenging and rigorous assignment to serve with the United Nations (UN) International Police Task Force (IPTF), as international police monitors (IPMs), for one year.

Aside from the excessive use of acronyms, it sounded intriguing.

Qualifications:
- US Citizen
- Minimum eight (8) years full-time sworn civilian police service to include patrol training/experience. Must have been active within the last five (5) years. Military service may partially substitute for civilian police experience. Preference will be given to officers who are currently on active duty.
- Ability to communicate in English
- Valid US Driver's License and ability to drive 4 x 4 vehicle
- Unblemished background record

Apparently, getting accepted was going to be the easy part. The tough part was the decision to go so far away from my kids.

I cooked up a family favorite, known in the house as Chicken Parisian—chicken breasts sautéed with mushrooms, garlic, and sour cream—and my three kids and I sat down at the dining-room table to talk it through. The oldest two, Jake and Sarah, were in college, and knew we could really use the extra money for tuition. My decision wouldn't directly impact them at this point; it was fifteen-year-old Erin who would be most affected by not having her mom around. Erin already lived with her dad, the result of a two-year-long, ugly custody battle. I knew my heartache would be the same whether I was in Nebraska or Bosnia, but for the first time in a while, here was something I was excited about, something I could believe in that would also put me in new surroundings, far away from the wreckage of my divorce.

"Mom," Jake began. "We want you to have this opportunity and you'd be out of the line of fire. Besides, we've seen you come home from work in bandages, on crutches—"

"And concussed," Sarah added.

"I know, I know," I said. Then I looked at Erin. She was trying to be as grown up as she could muster, but I could see tears welling in her eyes. "Mom," she said. "I know this is what you need to be doing."

And so I decided to give up certain comforts I took for granted— electricity on demand, toilets, walking down the street without fear of getting your legs blown off—and handed in my resignation letter to the chief of the Lincoln Police Department.

Police Chief Thomas Casady sent a letter back to me: "I don't want you to leave LPD. You are a fine officer, a valued employee, a good person, and a friend. We need you." He went on to explain that, after deep consideration, he would grant me a leave of absence for thirty days, during which time he hoped I would change my mind.

When I entered the chief's office to finalize my resignation, he gave me a long stare. Straightlaced and serious, he was one of the most exacting people I had ever known, which is why his response caught me off guard. He told me that I really did not want to go work with that bunch of idiots. At the time, I figured this was just his awkwardly endearing way of trying to say good-bye. I did not have any inkling that he might have known more than he was letting on—military contractors and companies like DynCorp were still a nascent breed, but perhaps the chief had heard reports from the field and had suspicions about what I getting myself into. I should have asked questions, but instead I just gave him a perplexed look. He reiterated that I had thirty days to change my mind. But I knew that wasn't going to happen. I was thirty-eight years old and needed change in my life. To me, this was the opportunity of a lifetime.

The truth was, most of my DynCorp colleagues had a personal story that compelled them to join the mission, whether they admitted to it or not. There had to be a pretty significant reason for someone at a later stage in his or her career to uproot without family and head 5,000 miles away. In one way or another, we were all running from something. But there is a difference between leaving and escaping. And some of my DynCorp colleagues were definitely escaping—taking cover in a place where no one knew of the very bad things they had done back home and where they thought no one would notice if they carried on, this time taking advantage of a broken people and a broken system.

2

STOP THE THREAT
(The Early Years–June 1999)

I was born a Bolkovac, a not-uncommon name in Croatia but one that always required me to spell it out in Nebraska. All I knew of my family history was that my grandfather, John Bolkovac, left Croatia when he was sixteen. He eventually found work in the steel mill in Youngstown, Ohio, met and married a U.S.-born woman with Croatian roots, and raised five sons. There was little talk about our heritage, and the only time I ever heard my grandfather mention the old country was when he visited our farm and compared the Nebraska countryside to his home, Vukovar Gorica, a farming community outside of Zagreb. Although my grandfather's generation spoke Croatian, his sons were never taught the language. "You are American, you speak English," he would say. He created a truly all-American family: his sons all went to college and were all outstanding football players, with my dad and uncle going on to play for Pitt, Army, and the Steelers.

My parents met on a blind date while Dad was at University of Pittsburgh and Mom was attending Kent Sate; they eloped not long thereafter. Mom, originally from Ohio, had lived in South Africa for several years when her father, a manager for Goodyear Tire and Rubber, helped open the first plant there. Like my father, she had grown up in an athletic family. Her father had managed to letter in football, basketball, track, and baseball while at Ohio State University—he had also been homecoming king and crowned an amateur model for his queen; she would go on to become his wife.

The two generations of women in my life, on both my parents' sides, ranged in personality from strong-willed to forces to be reckoned with. These women were the loudest voices at any sporting event. They taught me to do a job right the first time, that it was okay to speak out, and that you should always have a soft spot for the underdog.

My first nickname was Fireplug, given to me by my uncle Nick. Yes, my dad agreed, she has got our linebacker shoulders. Given Uncle Nick's and Dad's football careers, I was flattered—as only a kid could be—to have inherited their stout, broad frame. I was strong like them, and this too was a trait my family enjoyed pointing out.

One day, when I was about twelve years old, Mom and I hopped into the pickup truck, with the lawnmowers still in the back, to make a milk run. In my hometown of Douglas—thirty miles outside the Nebraska state capital, with a population of 100—this meant heading to the local bar. The Pony Express served as watering hole, gossip central, and mini mart; you could get milk, eggs, and butter along with your Pabst. A handful of farmers were there playing pitch and poker, and after Mom bought our groceries, she announced, "Anyone want to arm wrestle Kathy? She just beat all the boys down at the house." I imagine the farmers, at first, thought it was cute and that they would pretend to put up a good fight before kindly letting me win. Instead, Mom and I left all of them red-faced and asking, "What the hell is in that milk?"

As far back as I can remember, I always liked hard, physical work. As a kid, if I got to spend all day working the farm and could come in dirty and sweaty and hungry, I felt a sense of accomplishment.

My dad was an industrial engineer and while our 360-acre farm was his hobby, it was my mom who essentially ran the place, tending daily to the cattle, horses, chickens, pigs, and cutting and baling hay. Mom also drove the morning school bus and worked part time as a bank teller.

My two sisters and I were born in three consecutive years; ten years later my brother would come along. The classic middle child, I was the peacekeeper between my older sister, Betsy, who was the overachiever, and my younger sister, Carrie, the troublemaker. I was a chubby tomboy who liked playing football with the boys. In my teens, volleyball became the center of my world, and I made the Junior Olympic team and earned a full athletic scholarship to the University of Houston. But after six weeks of college, I came back home to marry my first and only boyfriend. It rained ice on the November day of my wedding and, as I was about to walk down the aisle of St. Martin's Roman Catholic Church, my dad whispered to me, "It's not too late to change your mind." For what seemed the first time, I did not listen to his advice. By the time I was twenty-three years old, I was a mother of three. The years went by, the kids became our lives, and my husband and I realized we did not have much else in common.

My first career was in the hotel industry, and I worked my way up to management at the Holiday Inn Crowne Plaza in Houston. Hotel management was a very different world from where I would end up, but the signs of my future path were there, such as the adrenaline rush I felt when I turned down the bed in the celebrity suite, booked by a heavy metal band, and found a sawed-off shotgun under the pillow; or the time the fire alarm went off and I hurdled the front desk—in heeled pumps—to radio security and assemble the quick response team.

My divorce—the first divorce in my extended family—came after ten years of pretending everything was okay. For the first time in my life, I felt like a failure. It was then that I happened on a newspaper ad for open positions in the Lincoln Police Department. I was familiar with guns, having gone on hunting trips with my dad, and I was a diehard fan of cop shows like Matlock, Magnum P.I., Police Woman, and Perry Mason. This was a world I wanted to be a part of.

————

From the moment I sat down for my first interview at the Lincoln police station in 1989, I felt as if my life was starting over and that this was where I belonged. Many of the officers were farmers' sons and former football players, and it was in this wholesome mix of athleticism, smarts, and discipline that I felt most comfortable. My initial interview was with Sergeant Jim Hawkins, who would go on to have a profound effect on me as a police officer and as a person. Hawk had played football at the University of Nebraska, and while he possessed a no-nonsense attitude, he was genuinely interested in and concerned for his officers and was always available for advice and mentoring. I will never forget leaving that interview and thinking that Hawk was just about the coolest person I had ever met.

After undergoing the routine physical and psychological tests, a polygraph, and numerous personal interviews, I was recruited for the force and started at the police academy. I naturally took to the qualification courses—running and diving (volleyball all over again), wrestling on floor mats with the guys as we learned takedown techniques, climbing barricades and walls, and shooting. At close range, I was a good shot, landing bullets in the target silhouette's head and center mass. But somewhere between fifteen and fifty yards, a particularly bad habit set in: I could not place my shots anywhere but the ball-bag. I would aim for center mass, but my bullets invariably landed groin high, obliterating any indication that my cardboard target may have had testicles. While Freud would have had a distinct view of the situation, I swore to my colleagues I was no man-hater. Just a heavy trigger pull, I would justify. They would feign agreement, then cough out "ball buster" under their breath.

I graduated from the State of Nebraska Law Enforcement Academy and earned my commission, badge, and gun. Soon enough, I was bestowed with another nickname. My beat partner and I were about to make an arrest, but the suspect refused to get out of his car. He had a vise grip on the steering wheel, requiring me to extract him forcibly. As I pulled him down to the ground so I could cuff him, he craned his neck to yell to my partner, "Who is this woman, Xena the Warrior Princess?" My partner, who had been standing there watching me wrestle the guy, burst out laughing. In my ten years at the station, I never lived that moment down.

I spent my first couple of years as a cop on the street, and then I turned my focus to domestic abuse cases and child sex crimes. I took courses and national seminars to become certified in forensic science technology, crime scene management, and advanced interview and interrogation techniques. I was placed on the Youth Aid unit, now known as the Special Investigations Unit, and, in my three years there, made over sixty felony arrests and had a 95 percent conviction rate of predators of women and children.

The scope of my job began to change dramatically when gang violence moved into Lincoln. My beat was the wrong side of the tracks: southwest Lincoln, where the Hatfields and McCoys were alive and kicking. I would respond to calls that shotguns were jutting from the windows of households as people were shooting at each other from across the street, or that entire families were in the middle of the street dueling with baseball bats. Then there were the emotionally charged domestic-in-progress calls—usually between spouses or couples—which were the most unpredictable and therefore the most dangerous. I was injured several times; the most serious injury was when my partner and I made an arrest on the third floor of an apartment building and were jumped from behind as we were escorting the cuffed detainee down the stairs. I went flying down two flights and knocked my head at the bottom. Code 61 went out over the radio—OFFICER NEEDS IMMEDIATE ASSISTANCE—requiring an all-out red lights-and-sirens response from every single available unit. I arrived home to my kids in the early hours of the morning. My stitched-up head was wrapped in bandages and I limped in on crutches for my sprained ankle. "Bad day, huh, Mom?" Jake asked. We were scheduled to spend the day at Worlds of Fun amusement park, and I was not going to let my kids down. *What concussion?* I jokingly asked myself as the first roller coaster climbed up and up—and then threw up the whole way down, much to the mortification of my kids.

Then came the day—after nine years on the street—that most cops train their entire career for but hope they will never have to encounter. It was early afternoon, and, just coming on duty, I was dispatched to a domestic assault in progress. Since it was during our shift change, no backup was available yet. I proceeded alone to the scene, a dilapidated area known as the German and Russian Bottoms, which, as the name implies, had long ago swelled with European immigrants. As I drove up the block, there was commotion on a front lawn, and a man was bleeding as if an artery were spurting. Two other people had gathered and when they saw me, they furiously pointed down the street. There I caught a flash of man hightailing it around the corner. I radioed dispatch to get medical and to send more units and then hit the pedal of my Chevy Tahoe in pursuit.

The station had just bought these new Tahoes, and I affectionately referred to mine as my Urban Assault Vehicle. Although other officers preferred their sedans, I liked my truck—at stoplights I could peer down into people's cars and see them drinking beer or lighting up something illegal. I was used to driving pickups and tractors, so I knew how to really maneuver a truck, and as I tracked the suspect, I was able to keep a good eye on him. Every time he looked back, he saw my roaring, oversized engine barreling down after him, driving on sidewalks when I had to.

When he climbed over a backyard fence, I was forced to abandon my truck and give foot pursuit. I chased him over more fences and throughout a maze of back streets. Eventually, gasping for breath, we ended up within a few feet of each other in the dead end of a desolate alley.

He turned on me and pulled a switchblade. I backed away a few steps while drawing my duty weapon.

"Drop the knife, you are under arrest," I said.

He grunted. "You want some, bitch?" Then he lunged, thrusting the knife at me.

I pulled the trigger. I heard the pop, but the suspect did not go down. Instead, he raised his hand above his head and launched the knife at me. I quickly darted off the line and fired again. This time he turned, took a couple of wobbly steps, then stumbled to the ground. I could see blood beginning to seep through his clothes. Unflinching, I stood with my weapon still aimed on him.

Sirens grew closer and cars screeched behind me, and I heard a steady voice say, "Go ahead and holster your gun, Kath."

Backup continued to respond from around the city, and everything seemed to move in slow motion as my sergeant drove me to the station. I was given a new gun while mine was taken into evidence for the standard internal investigation.

The suspect lived and gave a full confession: He was on parole for armed robbery, was a gang member, was HIV-positive, and had been drinking alcohol throughout the day while watching a violent movie. He had beaten his girlfriend and small baby (the 911 domestic call I had originally responded to), then had fled the house, stabbing an innocent man in passing (miraculously, the victim survived). That was when I happened to arrive.

I took a couple of days off to recuperate from the trauma, then resumed my duties the following week. My fellow officers were none too quick to let me know just how great of a shot I was. Xena, Warrior Princess had struck again, they said. Training and defensive tactics to "stop the threat" consist of two rapid-fire shots, a pause, then a third shot. The sequence is referred to as "two to the body, one to the head." In high-stress situations, well-trained officers will revert back to this training sequence, even if they are not necessarily conscious of it. And that is exactly what happened with me: Although I thought I had fired only two shots, three bullets had left my gun. The bullet to the head had missed, one bullet lodged in the rib cage, and the other, of course, was strategically placed in the man's groin.

———

When you are in a life-threatening situation, images pass before your eyes. It was my children's faces I saw, and it began happening more and more often. Every time I would get detailed to a call in progress, I would think of my kids, and I knew this meant it was time to make a change. I still wanted to be in law enforcement, but I needed to step away from the direct line of fire.

It was at this point when I saw the ad on the bulletin board in the station.

3

COPS FOR HIRE
(April–June 1999)

DynCorp sent me a packet of information and the request to fax back references, along with answers to a written psychological exam. Then a DynCorp staffer called and gave me the dates of the weeklong training session in Fort Worth, Texas, after which I would be issued a contract. From there, the training class would depart to Bosnia.

So that's it, I wondered, *I'm in? No in-person interview?* Since this was a company representing the State Department, I had expected to be put through extensive background checks. The process felt skewed—the little information DynCorp had requested seemed inadequate to properly assess candidates' qualifications, and if the actual selection was to occur just before our departure overseas, were candidates expected to have already quit their current jobs? At the time, I assumed that all candidates would, like me, be currently employed by a police department.

No matter; I was well qualified and the references DynCorp solicited were solid. Given that this application process was hardly as rigorous as the one for the Lincoln Police Department, I was not worried about getting the job. In early June 1999, my friends from the force threw me a little going-away party, I traded in my car for a compact car that my daughter Sarah could take to college, packed up my duffel bags with a year's worth of necessities, and said tight-throated goodbyes to my kids at the airport.

————

I was surprised to learn that the DynCorp training headquarters in Fort Worth were in rented space in an American Airlines building. The surprises would not stop there. I had assumed that I would be working with elite officers from all over the United States; instead, the people lining up for registration could be divided into two distinct groups: youngsters whose pimply faces and braggadocio made it hard to believe they had the minimum requirement of eight years' active police experience, and the retiree set, sporting gray hair and pot bellies. One nice gentleman confessed to me that he was seventy-one years old.

Most of the recruits seemed to know someone who had been on a previous DynCorp mission and, with the help of a $250 referral fee, had been highly encouraged to apply. Many of them hailed from small southern towns, where they had been the chief of police of one- or two-man departments. They had never seen paychecks larger than $20,000 a year and were in blissful disbelief that they would be making $85,000—tax free. They spoke of the pay as if they had discovered gold.

The prevailing conversation as we waited was about weaponry, with the younger set egging on the older ones: "Do you think we'll get to train the locals on the big guns?" "How about on explosives?" "I hope we can teach the locals a thing or two about the use of force!"

I wanted to butt in and say, "If you had a clue you would have heard there was a recent war, and the locals already know a thing or two about guns, ammo, and sniper activity." But it was only the first day, so I kept my mouth shut.

Their jabber quickly turned into a round robin of, what else, their perfect dream gun: a .357 Magnum converted to a semiautomatic. With a hairpin trigger pull. And loaded with armor-piercing or, how about, hollowpoint, copper-tipped rounds for maximum impact and internal destruction of the target. And, of course, with a switch for instant conversion to a Taser gun with infrared night sight.

At that point, I could not take it anymore. "Hey," I said, "isn't anyone interested in the democratization of a country? Or in rebuilding community-based policing?" Judging from the blank stares, I was the only one.

This group was to be just a portion of the DynCorp contingent, so I reassured myself that this was just lousy timing, and, once in Bosnia, I would surely meet Americans who were highly trained and professional.

———

Eventually, during our week of training, I did come across a few officers who seemed to share my experience and goals. One was a woman from Florida named Venetta, who was in her forties and had good police training and experience in vice, drug, and prostitution undercover work. She also had kids back home. Her boyfriend was currently a contractor in a DynCorp mission in East Timor, and she seemed clued in on what to expect, a good person for me to stick around.

As our week-long training session went on, some of the older candidates were rejected for elevated blood pressure. A couple other people were sent home after the urine tests, a few more after the psychological evaluation. My evaluation entailed a five-minute conversation with a man whose qualifications were not cited and who concluded the interview by asking if I was interested in a management position within DynCorp. I answered that I would rather get some training on the ground first.

Not surprisingly, our group did not lose many candidates after the physical agility tests, which included a timed, 200-yard run that—conveniently for those with pacemakers—was downhill. Another agility test we underwent was to reach above our heads, then squat for thirty seconds, then touch our fingers to our noses with our eyes closed—not much different from a drunk driving test, and as I watched the others it looked as if there could have been some drunks.

On the last night of our training session, a handful of us gathered by the swimming pool to share some beers. We pretty much assumed we would all see contracts the next day and figured we should get to know each other since we would be spending the next year together. A Southern drawl burst through our small talk, and we turned to see a man who had introduced himself on the first day as Jim from Mississippi.

"Hi y'all!" Jim called. "Don't start the party without me." Jim had greasy gray hair and tobacco-stained teeth and was wearing nothing but swimming trunks, which showcased a beach-ball belly and stark white legs. He tromped straight to the beer, then splashed his way into the pool, all the while telling us that he had already been on one peacekeeping mission in Bosnia and had liked it so much he was signing on for another year. Then, in the same sentence in which he described how scenic Bosnia was, he said, "And I know where you can get really nice twelve- to fifteen-year-olds." The hum of the pool heater filled the awkward silence that followed. The others glanced around, then looked at me, the only woman in the group. All I could do was cock my head and give Jim from Mississippi an odd stare. I must have misheard, or perhaps missed a part of the conversation that would have somehow put his comment into context. I tried to convince myself that this had to be the case. It must be the case, because any other alternative would not only be repulsive but wildly illegal. Besides, DynCorp—now riding high on its coveted position as one of the largest government contractors—certainly would not have renewed the contract of a boasting pedophile. Conversation quickly resumed; the others, like me, must have brushed off the comment as too preposterous to be true. But I filed it away, hoping I would never see the day when I would make sense of it.

Out of a training class of fifty, forty-two of us made the final cut. We had lined up to receive our vaccinations when I heard Jim from Mississippi again. Laughing boisterously, he asked the nurse if she would oblige him with a shot for the clap.

We were fitted with used, dark blue uniforms with a patch of the American flag on the shoulder, and then light blue UN berets were passed out. I watched as most of the men pulled the beret on as they would a ski cap, down over their ears. After a training video about the war in Bosnia and a public relations plug about the important work DynCorp does for the government, we were given a strong plea to take advantage of the $250 referral fee and recommend a friend to DynCorp. Don't worry if your friend doesn't have eight years of active police duty, we were told—in order to fully staff this mission, DynCorp was waiving some of the minimum standards, including reducing the required number of active years of police service down to five (and, I later discovered, the company had completely removed the qualification of "unblemished background record" from the recruiting flier).

At last, we lined up to sign our contracts, and, with a "Make the State Department proud" farewell, off we were sent.

―――――

Apparently, I had stood out as a responsible member of our training class because, just before we left, I was named the group leader, in charge of overseeing our travel to Bosnia. In reality, all this meant was that I was the baby-sitter, herding stragglers and reprimanding pranksters, and that I had the privilege of using my personal credit card every time our travel arrangements got screwed up. Which was often.

Given the hundreds of millions of dollars DynCorp had been awarded from the U.S. government for this mission, a strikingly insufficient amount was allocated for getting us smoothly—and safely—to our destination. Amazingly, it took three full days of travel to get to the Balkans, with the delays starting before we even left Texas: we were told that the old Russian military airliner that DynCorp had chartered for the flight was rejected by the FAA. I was now having serious concerns about this company, but I kept telling myself things would be different when I arrived in Bosnia and started doing meaningful work with officers from around the world.

Eventually, we were booked on a commercial flight to New York. From there we had to be bused to another airport to catch a flight to London and, from there, another flight to Zagreb, Croatia (cheaper than flying straight into Sarajevo, apparently), where we were loaded onto two beat-up, bullet-ridden, dank buses with cracked windows, no air conditioning, no toilet, and no underneath storage for our luggage. Sitting on our suitcases and duffel bags, we rolled along for 180 miles—which took an unbelievable sixteen hours, after factoring in the mountain terrain, single-lane roads, no toilet on the bus, and lapses under the baking sun to repair several bus breakdowns. We had plenty of time to ruminate on how we had been treated so far. Although no one expected first-class travel, the word floating around the mission was that DynCorp had received $250,000 to $300,000 per monitor from the U.S. government; certainly this allowed for sensible travel arrangements.

Backdropped against the lush landscape, we rumbled past wagons full of vagrant families, known as Roma, or Gypsies; skin-and-bone goats tied to posts; and little children dressed in rags, begging along the roadside. The people of Bosnia had seen death and destruction that I could not imagine. That is also what had brought me here—I had watched from my sofa in Lincoln as the news relayed the slaughter, the orphans, the mass exodus. I could see the likeness of my grandparents in the faces of the old men and women helplessly bearing witness to the destruction of their families. I knew I had distant relatives there, enduring the terror, and I had a premonition that I would make my way to that part of the world someday.

We finally arrived in Sarajevo, only to be informed by DynCorp supervisors that, unfortunately, the $90 per diem we were contracted to get paid had been reduced to $75. One man quit right then and there, declaring that DynCorp had been nothing but dishonest so far. I watched as he thrust over his blue beret and contemplated whether I should do the same. But here I was, finally in the middle of Bosnia. Yes, DynCorp had misrepresented itself and definitely had some competence issues—and by now it owed me a sizable amount for my charged-up credit card—but all around me were the survivors of a horrendous war, the torment still visible in their eyes.

This was a country that exhaled desperation but inhaled perseverance. I was not ready to just turn around and go home.

4

SARAJEVO
(June 1999)

We were set up in a hotel in the northern hills of Sarajevo. First thing the next morning, a bus wound us down the narrow, cobbled street into the city center for our weeklong orientation session. We rolled down the main road, Boulevard Meše Selimovića, better known as Sniper Alley during the siege, when the Serbs held the entire capital city hostage. This street, the only way in and out of the city, was vulnerable to the row of high-rise buildings and hillside houses, where snipers would wait and peck off innocent civilians, especially children. The scars in the concrete left by exploding shells had now been filled in with red resin that formed flowerlike shapes referred to as Sarajevo roses, in remembrance of the person who had been shot at that spot.

We arrived at a nondescript, aged UN building dubbed Tito Barracks, after the former leader of Yugoslavia, Josip Broz Tito, whose presidential term had spanned three decades. This was the training facility where the weeklong orientation for all new monitors arriving from UN participating countries took place. The building housed some UN offices as well. A new site was under construction to the west of the barracks and would be completed in a year.

Surrounded by stone walls, barbed wire fence, and armed guards perched in lookouts on the roof, Tito Barracks was not exactly the most welcoming place. Its yards were wild and overgrown, but on closer inspection, I saw this was not due to neglect—the wrangled, rusted metal rims of land mines were visible, poking through the ground. Because of this, designated walkways were cordoned off for us to enter and exit the building.

The sight of refugees around Sarajevo, old and young, hobbling around on one leg, was an immediate and consistent reminder that mines still infested the area. The mines had been hidden everywhere—from public squares to private gardens, where, in between the vegetables, they had been planted by the man of the house who would have rather had his home blown up than had it taken from him.

At Tito Barracks we joined our new colleagues: the International Police Task Force (IPTF), a melting pot of nearly two thousand civilian police officers from forty-five UN countries. Despite the fact that we all came from dramatically different cultures and held startlingly different views on policing, we all cheerily donned our berets and our IPTF uniforms with the UN badge on one shoulder and the flag of our home country on the other.

DynCorp rotated out officers approximately every six months, or as positions opened up on an as-needed basis. I was encouraged by the caliber of some Americans I met, and I struck up conversations with several men and women who had backgrounds and educational levels similar to mine (even though I had left school to get married, I went to the University of Nebraska and took other college courses while working as a police officer). Because they had already been in Bosnia for up to several months, they were eager to answer questions and give advice, and they all echoed a similar sentiment: The best jobs in the mission were basically desk jobs, with easy, routine work that kept your weekends open for travel through Europe.

I was all for travel and having fun, but I could not see myself spending the next year pushing paper. I wanted to have an active presence and work with the locals on building democracy and effective policing institutions. The truth was, I wanted to make a difference. But each time I explained this, I was met with the same general response: The less you become involved in trying to solve major issues, the happier you will be.

A couple of people suggested that if I was really interested in hands-on work while I was there, I should apply to the human rights division. It was never far from my mind that I gave up a good career in law enforcement to come here, so I submitted my request to the IPTF evaluation committee to work in human rights.

I was required to make a presentation on an area of my choosing within the field, and the deciding body would be the new-recruits panel, consisting of two European monitors, who supposedly had expertise in human rights issues. Standing before the two-man panel, I presented on sexual assault investigation and methods of evidence collection. About thirty seconds in, and coinciding with my use of the word "vaginal," the men turned red. As I described plucking pubic hairs from the suspect and the importance of documenting specific findings from the victim's medical examination, such as whether the hymen was intact if the victim was a child, I watched both men deepen in color and become fidgety. They could not have been more relieved when I concluded my presentation. They quickly conferred with whispers and nods and then scribbled something on my evaluation sheet and handed it to me. They had written: "A++."

I looked back to the two flushed men; they nodded hurriedly, motioning me to the door. I was now a human rights investigator.

Next I had to be recruited to a specific IPTF station somewhere in Bosnia that was in need of a human rights investigator. This recruiting practice was about as comprehensive as college sorority or fraternity rush, and it was also my first dose, on Bosnian soil, of the anything-goes attitude. During breaks from our classes, as we mingled in the halls, I felt like fresh meat being scrutinized by hundreds of monitors—mostly men—who had already completed half their mission time. It was all too obvious that the few of us women were the most sought-after recruits.

"I heard you're from Nebraska. What a small world, I am too!" a man named Harry said as he pumped my hand. He told me he was the deputy station commander in Ilidža, a western suburb of Sarajevo, and that he was about to be moved up to commander. He stressed that he really wanted me to come work in his station, which, he informed me, had the best parties in the mission.

Parties were not exactly on my list of criteria in choosing a station. "We'll see," I answered, and stepped back to watch as Harry went on to make the rounds with all the other new female monitors.

At the end of the week, the notification came that I—along with four other Americans, one of whom was Venetta—was assigned to the Ilidža station, where we would have the privilege of partaking in the best parties in the mission.

————

With orientation—which mostly consisted of talks about different aspects of the mission and speakers from various international organizations we would be working with on the ground—over, it was time for us to find our own living accommodations. Unlike the military, we were not confined to a base, and while NATO guidelines prohibited soldiers from stepping foot off base except for assigned patrols or special granted leaves, DynCorp monitors could come and go as we pleased, free to roam the country in white UN Land Rovers and Toyota 4-Runners (gassing up as often as we needed and for no charge at any designated fueling station or the NATO Stabilization Force—SFOR—military base). We could eat at restaurants, stay out until all hours, and cavort with the locals. We also accrued vacation time and could take road trips in our provided vehicles or take flights (on our own dime) throughout the continent on our days off.

Venetta and I, along with several other Americans, set out with a language assistant to hunt for living quarters. We were all concerned that, with our reduced per diem, we might have trouble finding something affordable, but it quickly became apparent that even with the cutback, we IPTF still had a great gig. Not only were we making base salaries with at least a percentage that was tax free (for us DynCorp contractors, 100 percent was tax free), but the cost of living in Bosnia did not even come close to the allotted $75 a day. Rent was between $200 to $400 a month per person—less if you lived outside Sarajevo—and food was cheap. A decent restaurant meal could cost as little as $2, and it cost only a few bucks to buy bread, fruit, and vegetables for the week. What was left over was more money than people from some participating countries— Ghana, Pakistan, and Romania, to name a few—had ever had their hands on and was far more than the average income in Bosnia, which was around $10 a day. The families that rented their homes to mission personnel greatly benefited from this additional income.

When we saw the farmhouse on the Vrelo Bosne, Venetta and I, along with our new roommates—Mike, a soft-spoken and polite guy from Illinois, who brought his folk guitar with him; and Weldon, a family man from Alabama, who talked a lot about his middle school–age sons—rented it immediately.

———

In preparation for my new job, I studied the materials we were given during orientation, including the mandate laid out in the Dayton Peace Agreement for human rights work. It was dizzying reading, as the branches, tiers, management, hierarchy, and the acronyms describing other acronyms were complex and often convoluted. Here are the basics: The Dayton Agreement established a Commission on Human Rights for Bosnia, composed of a high commissioner and a court chamber. The commission was authorized to investigate human rights violations, issue findings, and bring proceedings before the court; and the court was authorized to issue binding decisions. The commission was also responsible for working closely with the UN human rights agencies, the Organization for Security and Cooperation in Europe (OSCE), and other human rights groups, all of which were supposed to check and balance each other. Over time, the temporary chamber was taken over by the national courts, and most gender issues were monitored primarily by the UN Office of the High Commissioner for Human Rights (UNOHCHR).

My job technically fell under a few separate umbrellas. First, I was a civilian police monitor, working with the IPTF and contracted via DynCorp. Neither DynCorp nor its managers were part of the IPTF; rather, DynCorp was a corporate entity that handled payroll and most administrative and logistical issues for our basic needs, such as our monthly time sheets, mail service, bottled water, uniform replacement, and—my favorite part—a small canteen with VHS movies. (I am a John Wayne fanatic, and the canteen seemed to have nearly every movie he made.)

Second: For IPTF issues related to our working mandate in Bosnia, I reported to the IPTF chain of command—the highest rank being the IPTF police commissioner, a French general named Vincent Coeurderoy. The commissioner answered to the highest-ranking mission official: the UN Special Representative to the Secretary General (SRSG), an American diplomat named Jacques Paul Klein, who had been appointed by the UN secretary general, Kofi Annan.

It was highly common for DynCorp contractors to move up the IPTF hierarchy—and since the American contingent was nearly twice as large as that of any other nation, there were significantly more American contractors represented in the upper ranks. For example, the IPTF deputy commissioner reporting to Coeurderoy was a DynCorp contractor and former deputy chief of police from Colorado. Likewise, many of the regional and station commanders and key people in Internal Affairs and the organized crime unit were American DynCorp contractors. Adding to this, many of the contractors knew each other from back home (thanks to the enticing referral fee) so in my short time there it had already become apparent that, despite an international presence of thousands, the inner circle had swiftly become an insular American boys' club.

The real work I was to do in the mission, however, would fall under the third part of the umbrella: human rights, and I would be reporting to the UN Office of the High Commissioner on Human Rights, which was headed by a British attorney named Madeleine Rees. While there were a handful of American IPTF in human rights, the long days, overnight on-call hours, and often grueling work did not appeal to most of my peers, so I would be working primarily with internationals.

To make the division of branches even more confusing, there was some overlap in who did what job. For example, DynCorp handled payroll (our base salary of $45,000, along with a $5,000 mission completion bonus), but our $75 per diem, called our mission subsistence allowance, came from the UN personnel office and was a separate monthly payment. The UN staff and supervisors also managed and approved our leave requests, which we in turn documented on our DynCorp monthly time sheets.

While these various branches and overseeing bodies seemed, in theory at least, to balance power and authority, it was an incredible maze of people and departments and entities to sift through. Even those who had been there awhile still seemed somewhat confused about the various roles. A lieutenant general summed up the perpetual confusion and acronym soup like this: "I thought I knew all types of command and control that existed (OPCOM, OPCON, TACON, etc.), but my division commanders have managed to teach me three that I did not know. When I want my French division commander to do something that he disagrees with, he has the tendency to remind me that he is under 'OP NON.' My American division commander is a bit more blunt and asserts, 'OP NOWAY.' My fellow Brit is the height of courtesy and simply tells me 'OP YOURS!' "[1]

Several UN countries had both civilian police and military troops (which were part of SFOR) present in Bosnia, and the two were viewed as connected branches. This meant, for example, that the German, Turkish, Italian, and Dutch IPTF—all of whom were part of their national police forces or military back home—could visit their respective military bases for assistance and support, such as medical care. This was not the case with the United States. The American military, stationed on SFOR base camps throughout the country, were an entirely separate entity from us DynCorp contractors, and the military wanted it to stay that way.

We were not allowed to receive medical treatment on the U.S. base camp; rather, DynCorp offered an emergency medical care team, which was a couple of roving civilian medics, and attempts to successfully reach them on their mobile phones often took hours or even days. (At least for real medical emergencies we could rely on the German field hospital, where they would treat us for a small fee, or we went to local hospitals.) The only arrangement DynCorp could strike with the military was that we could enter a U.S. base camp to use the gym or to shop at the PX for American-brand groceries; however, these privileges were revoked periodically due to DynCorp contractors' disruptive behavior, such as sneaking into restricted areas or shoplifting. It quickly became clear why the military did not seem to want much to do with us and did not take kindly when locals assumed that DynCorp and the U.S. military were one and the same.

To better understand the country and what the people had been through, I paid a visit to the hauntingly sad Olympic Village in Sarajevo. Only several years before the siege, the city had been home to what Sports Illustrated called "the sweetest Winter Olympics of them all." Now the cheery "Welcome Sarajevo '84" sign depicting the cartoon Olympic mascot Vučko the wolf, touting skis under his paws, was riddled with bullets. Walking further into the village, I saw what happened when the Sarajevo cemeteries had overflowed: The Olympic soccer stadium had been turned into a mass gravesite with Popsicle stick–shaped planks serving as headstones, lining the field from goal to goal. Most graves were unmarked.

That night Venetta and I pampered ourselves with manicures and a late-night talk, centering on our kids, whom we missed desperately, and our love lives, which were nondescript. At 0800 we reported to the Ilidža IPTF station.

5

"ACCIDENTS" HAPPEN
(June–September 1999)

Bosnia consists of several regions, called cantons, and the Ilidža ITPF station was part of the Sarajevo Canton. The station sat on the main road that ran east to Sarajevo and west to the Croat-populated city of Kiseljak. A tourist destination for its thermal springs and mountain ski trails, Ilidža had been held by the Serbs during the war. During the siege, the three-mile, few-minute ride into the city along Sniper Alley was described by *New York Times* reporter John F. Burns as the dash you will never forget:

> Many spend hours or days preparing, calculating the least hazardous moment, emblazoning their vehicles with flags and stickers identifying them as foreigners, consulting with others who have made the journey, or waiting for a United Nations military convoy to follow…Ultimately, no amount of calculation eliminates the risks. A British officer completing a three-month tour…chuckled at the sight of reporters preparing their jeep with American and British flags. "Look," he said, "whether you make it or not depends on whether the sniper in that house by the road can be bothered to lift his rifle and fire or not, or whether he's napping."[1]

From our accommodations, Venetta and I effortlessly made the drive to the IPTF station, a building that had previously been a workshop and garage; the industrial elements of exposed pipes and non-insulated walls of its former existence remained.

Harry was there to greet Venetta, me, and a man who went by the nickname Gunny: the three new American recruits. We were then introduced to nearly twenty IPTF monitors from around the world and various language assistants. I moved through the group, shaking hands and trying to grasp the variety of foreign names. One man in particular took me off guard—a member of the Dutch contingent, with bright blue eyes and shoulders broad enough to eclipse my own linebacker frame. His handshake lingered as he introduced himself in impeccable English. "Hello, Jan Van der Velde, it is a pleasure to meet you." Our eyes locked until we realized that others were taking notice. Embarrassed, I stammered, "O-oh yes, pleasure to meet you as well," and quickly moved on, as Jan's confident smile trailed me.

I was relieved when I met the station's senior human rights investigator, Bo Andreasson, with whom I would be working closely. Bo, who had been in the mission for several months already, was a veteran officer from Sweden who held the Swedish rank of crime inspector. In his late forties, he had a wife and family in Malmo, one of Sweden's largest cities. I quickly learned that Bo was a famous storyteller, with a penchant for folktales. He and I immediately clicked. He was extremely bright, shared my sense of gallows humor, and was ready and charged to work hard—a rare quality, judging from the prevailing attitude during my orientation week.

Bo and I would be sharing an office, and I quickly noted that Jan's office was directly across from ours. Jan was already some steps ahead of me and was immediately at my service, hooking up my computer and phone wires, adjusting my chair, even building shelves next to my desk. Bo just sat back and watched with a big smile, then whispered to me—at least once a day: "It's all about energy, Kathryn." I appreciated Jan's help—it meant a lot to have someone like him looking out for me—but I learned he had only six weeks remaining before he returned home to the Netherlands and I wasn't interested in a meaningless mission fling. While I had dated since my divorce, I was hesitant to get seriously involved again, especially with someone from a foreign country.

————

During my first weeks at Ilidža, I became acquainted with standard operating procedure. The grand design of the IPTF was the coming together of police forces from every UN country to assist and train the Bosnian police after their homeland had been torn apart; however, this ambitious goal was continuously interrupted. Forget about training the locals; we first had to figure out how the IPTF could work together. There was incredible transience, with the constant beginning and ending of monitors' contracts; although English was the mandated language, the level of proficiency was often scarily low; the Ghanaian officers did not know how to drive, let alone handle the stick-shift UN vehicles; the Spanish forces would take siesta for a couple of hours smack in the middle of their shifts; other officers from less-developed countries had no idea how to collect evidence, interview victims or suspects, create a case file, or write a police report. It appeared that those of us from America and Western Europe would be spending as much time training other IPTF members as training the locals.

On the flip side, American and western European IPTF members needed to rethink many of our skills and the "right" way to do police work—the way we operated, with the aid of computers and other technology, was simply not going to happen in Bosnia, where often the most advanced piece of equipment in police stations was a manual typewriter. There were many tasks I simply did not know how to perform—or at least perform effectively—without the necessary equipment. For example, American companies were sending over such things as expired rape kits in exchange for tax write-offs. The expiration date was hardly the issue: Even if we trained the local authorities how to collect a specimen, the stations had neither refrigerators in which to store the samples nor crime labs in which to analyze them.

One of the more frustrating tasks was dealing with housing issues. The goal was to reinstate families displaced by the war back into their homes. The problem was that house of the original owner was almost always occupied by a family that had bought it from another family that had bought it from those who had stolen the house. In order to reinstate one family, the IPTF had to put another family out on the street, when they had suffered the same fate: Some other family was occupying their home. Before the war, the population of Yugoslavia was made up of percentages of Bosniaks, Serbs, and Croats in distinct regions; after the war, these percentages had flip-flopped. Now, as some years had passed, everyone was unsure how to get back to the way things were, especially after new roots had started taking hold. It was like a game of musical houses, where the IPTF was stuck taking the needle on and off the record player, then left to deal with the odd people out.

These exercises in futility now made it clear why I had been forewarned that the less I tried to accomplish, the happier I would be. It was no secret that as long as we monitors checked in at the duty station, we could set our own work hours. Many of my colleagues, especially those doing routine jobs, such as monitor on patrol—otherwise referred to as "taking in the scenery"—equated simply being dressed in a UN uniform for eight hours with putting in a full day's work.

————

It was not long before Harry threw one of his famous parties. Any excuse was good enough—someone's birthday, someone's mission time ending—to fill the station with beer kegs, tubs of liquor, endless barbecue, and blasting music. Everyone was invited, from the language assistants to folks from regional headquarters. I was introduced to two high-ranking DynCorp contractors: the IPTF Sarajevo regional commander and the IPTF advisor to Sarajevo's minister of the interior, Roy. Roy described his close relationship with the minister, who oversaw public security and the police for the Sarajevo canton, and flaunted how he was invited to the minister's home for lavish family dinner parties. Roy also had been requested to provide training to the Bosnian Special Weapons Unit, a sort of SWAT team, which was headed by the minister's nephew.

I soon made my way toward Jan and Bo, and was entertained for the rest of the evening with Bo's folksy jokes:

It's shortly after World War II. The setting is a retirement home for women. Old Sven, who was an ace fighter pilot in the war, was giving a talk to the Ladies' Club about his experiences. "So dere I vas, at 13,000 feet...about a half hour from our target," Sven says, "vhen all of a sudden, I looked and saw some fokkers down below us. Ve started to dive....I hit tree tousand feet, an' dis fokker, he vas right on my tail." At this point, the chairwoman of the club interrupted and said, "I should probably inform all the ladies that a 'fokker' was a type of German airplane." Old Sven replied, "Ya, dat's right, but deze fokkers were flying Messerschmidts."

At the end of the night, Jan chivalrously walked me to my car, an old Land Rover I had been assigned. All the way down the street we could hear the music pounding and smell the barbecue wafting from the station. I wondered what the locals thought of all this.

Over the next several weeks, Bo, Jan, and I spent a significant amount of time together. During the days, Bo and I would do our fieldwork, visiting refugee camps to monitor that conditions were satisfactory and that there were no signs of abuse. This work was all relative, of course. The truth was that the conditions were rough: extreme overcrowding, fights breaking out with regularity, and police who were overly forceful while intervening. A major issue was the recent influx of Albanians fleeing across the border as war and bombing raged in Kosovo. The refugee camps were bursting at the seams, and resources were scarce enough that the children would stand at the roadside, in no shoes and dirty faces, selling candy or any other wares they could get their hands on.

After our long days trying to mediate many unsolvable issues, Bo, Jan, and I, along with some of their Dutch and Swedish colleagues, would get together for dinner. It was an interesting meld of cultures—the stories, the food, the jokes. Occasionally, one person would offer to cook up some regional dishes, but most times we went to a local restaurant that had picnic tables out back, called, simply, The Bar. We would order orange Cappys (a fruit soda; none of us drank on duty) and linger over The Bar's version of pizza. One of the waitresses took an immediate liking to Jan's roommate, Frenk. When her shift ended she would brazenly make her way to our table, slide onto the bench next to Frenk, and hang onto his arm for the rest of the night. Frenk was embarrassed by her overt attention and respectfully refused to take things any further. It was clear that many of the young women were desperately looking for a way out of Bosnia, or, as Jan would say, invoking military-speak for the convenience store at base camp: "They were out for a free ticket to the grand PX on the other side of the ocean."

A few weeks later, on the Fourth of July, it was my turn to entertain my international friends. I secured access to the nearby American base camp, Butmir, and Jan, Bo, Frenk, and I waited at the gates as guards hovered mirrors that looked like mammoth-size dentist's tools under our UN truck to search for bombs. After we were waved through, soldiers handed us little American flags to wave, and upon spotting a festive soldier dressed top hat to toe as Uncle Sam, we posed for a picture, barbed wire fences framing us in the background and rusted, mangled barricades in the foreground. At dusk, fireworks went off, and we oohed and ahhed over the show.

Soon, however, Jan's mission time in Bosnia came to an end, and we gathered at his house for farewell drinks. I was inside while the men were out by the grill supervising dinner, when through an open window I overheard Jan asking Bo to take good care of me and watch over me. I was stopped cold; it was at that moment when I felt certain I had fallen in love with Jan. But I quickly stifled the feeling—he would be gone the next day. Although we had grown close, Jan was in the process of getting divorced and had two young sons. I knew from experience how rough the situation could get. Chances that two divorced parents from two different countries and two different continents would even manage to see each other again were slim.

The next morning we cheered as Jan and his fellow Dutch officers, wearing pressed light blue shirts, black pants, and blue berets, received their medals for service from the Dutch contingent commander. Then they boarded a bus headed to the airport, where a military plane would return them to the Netherlands. I watched as the bus drove off, hoping that no one would notice I was crying.

———

That day, back at the station, Bo and I opened a particularly interesting human rights case. Harry had called Bo and me into his office and said that he and his language assistant had been walking down the street when they witnessed two men the assistant had recognized as alleged local mafia assault a local police officer. According to Harry, additional local police—the Policija—showed up and took the two men into custody, but when Harry was asked to provide a witness statement, he refused, claiming he did not want to put his language assistant in danger of retaliation from the suspects since she was present at the scene. Bo and I exchanged glances while Harry relayed the story; what kind of a police officer refused to provide a witness statement?

Harry went on to say he had been informed that the alleged criminals had been released from custody without proper authorization. In the few beats of silence that followed, I wondered what he wanted us to do about it. Bo and I volunteered to go to the local police station and find out what had happened. Harry seemed relieved—but to me it was not necessarily because justice was being served; it was more like he would sleep better that night.

It did not take us long to learn that the two men were still in custody and, looking to do a thorough day's work, Bo and I received permission to talk with them. One of the men owned a local restaurant in the Sarajevo suburb of Hadžići, and he was eager to tell us that the Sarajevo Ministry of the Interior was corrupt. I gave them the phone number to the Ilidža IPTF station and assured him that we would be interested in hearing any serious complaints of criminal activities, including activities within the government.

A week later my home phone rang just as I was about to get into bed. The caller introduced himself in broken English as the man we had talked to in the prison last week. He said he had been released and was at his restaurant earlier that night when, in the middle of a music concert, Policija officers in bulletproof vests, their faces masked with ski caps, stormed in and beat him and numerous patrons. He believed the men were officers from the Special Support Unit. I asked him for his mobile number, said I would be back in touch, and then immediately called Bo.

"Your home phone?" Bo said wearily. "Did someone at the IPTF station lose the security regulations?"[2]

"They'd have to first find the security regulations," I said. Despite the hour, Bo headed to the IPTF station so that he could follow protocol and return the man's call from an IPTF line, take an official statement, and fax it as a flash report—indicating a potentially serious situation had occurred—to IPTF Regional HQ in Sarajevo. According to the statement, the restaurant owner believed the raid was in retaliation for comments he had made about the minister of the interior being involved in cigarette smuggling—he knew of the smuggling because he admittedly had also been involved. "They were beating me more than an hour," he said. "I am afraid for my life and existence of my family. They were striking me in the back, kidneys, chest. They were saying 'We f____ your unborn child, you shall forget who was smuggling cigarettes.'"[3]

The next morning several other victims from the restaurant showed up to the IPTF station, and all gave statements detailing police brutality. That night the story made the local TV news, with victims showing evidence of their beatings.

The first thing that was clear to Bo and me was that the raid had breached protocol. According to UN mandate, any raid was to be conducted jointly by the Bosnian Policija and the IPTF. Instead, the Special Support Unit had launched the raid without involving the IPTF at all.

We also learned that the Policija had tried to cover up the raid, going so far as to have hospital personnel destroy records of people who had sought treatment for injuries. Finally, we confirmed that the Special Support Unit was headed by the nephew of the Sarajevo minister of the interior.

It was no secret that corruption and smuggling were rampant within the government—one IPTF head consistently referred to the country as a "nationalist kleptocracy."[4] The Policija were just as corrupt, albeit for slightly different reasons. To begin with, it was common knowledge that the mentality of the local police was not a universal desire "to serve and protect" but a specific "to serve and protect one's own kind." While the IPTF's job was to integrate the police force and mitigate discrimination, the wounds of ethnic cleansing were not just going to heal and disappear.

Despite these deep-rooted issues, there was a more basic problem: Not only were the local police meagerly paid, but often their pay was delayed because of lack of government funds. These delays could last up to several months. Graft was often too irresistible and too necessary to pass up. Regardless of political or financial motives, however, this case showed direct evidence of excessive use of force resulting in human rights violations.

The case was classified and assigned by the Regional Human Rights Office to Bo and me. I went to the Hadžići police station and requested copies of the custody records, so that we could have some type of corroborating evidence that an incident and arrest had occurred, but was told to come back later the next day. This was not acceptable, and I stood firm in requesting the copies—immediately. A couple of hours later, I finally walked out of the station, records in hand, although the file was in bad shape, barely documenting the essentials, such as the reason for arrest.

Back at the IPTF station, the advisor to the Hadžići Policija informed me that he had just received a call from the chief of the Hadžići station stating neither Bo nor I were welcome there anymore. "Inform the chief that I will take that under advisement and will be happy to send an incident report to Main HQ, recommending the Hadžići police chief be decommissioned. That this is our job, and they are going to have to comply with the mandates set out in the Dayton Agreement," I instructed the advisor, but he just gave me a blank stare.

Our next step would be to interview the head of the Special Support Unit that had launched the unauthorized raid—the minister's nephew. Immediately, DynCorp officer Roy, who had bragged to me at Harry's party about his relationship to the minister, came to mind, and Bo agreed that we should first go to Roy for guidance. We approached Roy in the hall at Sarajevo Regional Headquarters to request a meeting. Roy said he was already aware of the Hadžići incident, then he gave me a friendly nudge, trying to persuade me that the whole thing was not a big deal. "We all get out there and rub elbows a little bit at times, don't we?" he said.[5]

Bo and I were taken aback by Roy's cavalier attitude. We had collected significant evidence, including numerous victim statements, photographs of injuries, and a shirt with bloodstains and a large footprint (which appeared to have been made from a boot). The more witness statements that were taken, the more it appeared that those responsible for the unauthorized raid at least had connections with the Sarajevo Ministry of the Interior.

Around this time, the attitude of our station commander, Harry, began to change dramatically. Although many of the monitors took a serious interest in our case and asked us about new developments, Harry was disconcerted. Without prior communication, Harry switched Bo's schedule from a regular workweek to Tuesday through Saturday. Bo met with Harry to explain that the new schedule made the human rights work ineffective, as losing Mondays would not only compromise productivity but also would create unnecessary problems in compiling the comprehensive human rights report that was sent to Regional HQ every Wednesday.

Harry rose from his chair and yelled at Bo to get the hell out of his office. A few days later, at our regular morning meeting, Harry suggested, in front of the entire staff, that Bo and I were becoming overly involved in the Hadžići case and that our impartiality was in question.

"Harry, aren't we here to investigate internal corruption?" I asked.

Harry leaned in close. "I think you should back off a bit," he said. He then warned, in a concerned tone, that car accidents happen around here all the time—air-quoting the word "accidents." Bo and I looked at each other in disbelief. We were supposed to be enforcing the law, not letting the local mafia enforce their law on us.

I wrote Harry off as being miffed because Bo and I had stopped showing up to his parties, but Bo was stymied by the change in Harry. In the several months that Bo had been at the Ilidža station, he and Harry had gotten along well. Just after Harry's promotion to station commander, he had even asked Bo to be his deputy commander. Bo had respectfully declined, on the grounds that he was more interested in doing investigative work. Soon after, when the human rights position opened up at the station (just before I arrived), Harry assigned it to Bo. "Harry had asked me to go with him to Tito Barracks for lunch when your U.S. contingent arrived," Bo told me. "He'd said he heard there were some really good-looking women recruits."

I rolled my eyes, remembering how obvious Harry had been. Bo winked at me. "Well, he was right. Harry had such a proud smile the day he walked into the station with you and Venetta."

"Glad he has his priorities straight," I said.

———

It was the middle of August and it had been a week since Jan had left. One day, while discussing the Hadžići case in Bo's office, Jan called Bo's cell phone to check in from the Netherlands. Bo asked if I wanted to talk. I hesitated but couldn't help the tears from welling. Bo handed me the phone and left the room.

Jan told me he had gone for a long run and was calling from a pay phone. He was moving out of the house he shared with his wife and into his own apartment. We talked about the possibility of seeing each other again. I did not know what to say. I wanted to see him but did not want to be the woman who broke up his marriage. He assured me that was not the case. I knew most monitors had a story for why they came to Bosnia—this was Jan's.

————

After a few months, while I was still working the Hadžići case, all American monitors were requested to attend a contingent meeting to be held in Neum, Bosnia's only seaside town. Many monitors had to travel across the country to get to Neum, which jutted through Croatia to touch the Adriatic Sea. I envisioned a breathtaking coast with misty hilltops and desolate beaches; in reality, it was an abandoned tourist town, with rundown hotels and beaches covered in pebbles.

I thought the meeting would focus on issues relevant to the American contingent, such as how to best deal with other IPTF who did not have extensive police training or how to work around the lack of essential technology within local police stations. But instead it was a forum to complain and moan about our reduced per diem and lack of vacation days. Although there were a couple of self-congratulatory mentions of IPTF accomplishments, there was little to no discussion of current work issues or strategies. Important information was shared, however, about the opening of a new American-style casino in Sarajevo, outfitted with poker tables but not yet with blackjack or roulette.

A newsletter, edited and circulated by a DynCorp monitor, summarized the contingent meeting as "A great time was had by all!" and displayed scenic pictures of Neum as well as a lavish buffet with monitors lining up to eat. The newsletter also featured a message from the American contingent commander, Samuel K. Brown, whose own written summation of the meeting was:

"I believe overall, it went OK." Brown went on to detail a recent meeting he had with the highest-ranking mission officials, Special Representative to the Secretary General (SRSG) Jacques Klein, and the IPTF commissioner.

[Klein] is supportive of IPTF, but said in essence that we are our own worst enemies....The SRSG stated the he is seeing a lot of IPTF who are not behaving professional [sic] in their job performance, nor looking professional in appearance. By this he was referring to sloppy and dirty uniforms, long hair, beards and goatees....The SRSG also stated that many IPTF officers are not taking the mission seriously.

I could not have agreed more with the SRSG on this one: It was true that the Americans easily distinguished themselves, and not in a good way. Most UN IPTF members were part of their country's military force, and their pressed uniforms, at-attention stance, and physical fitness relayed this. The Americans, on the other hand, were private contractors who were considerably older, had their fair share of potbellies, and preferred street clothes to uniforms, or at the very least a combination of both.

The contingent commander went on to describe how "Again we screwed ourself [sic]" by stretching or breaking the rules and then complaining when privileges were revoked. He offered the example of the common, but improper, practice of allotting extra vacation days for travel time, so that monitors would take up to two extra days a month in paid leave to account for time traveling to the airport and flying to their vacation destination. He also included a copy of the letter he wrote to SRSG Klein as a follow-up to the meeting; it incorporated no future goals or vows to focus on specific issues but merely complained about the reduced per diem.

A note from the editor, which I felt was misguided, appeared on the final page of the newsletter. He wrote:

> I was very troubled after reading our Contingent Commander [Brown's] report on the meeting…with our new SRSG and Commissioner. I gave Commander Brown back his first draft and asked him to trim out about a dozen, "Violators will be repatriated" [sic]. Another overused phrase I suggested he reduce was, "IPTF monitors are their own worst enemy in this mission." Even after some extensive editing the report still comes off pretty hard.

———

Back at the Ilidža station after my seaside "getaway," Bo and I promptly decided to work our way up the ranks regarding the Hadžići case. Bo went to talk with the regional head of human rights, Stephen Bowen, a British attorney and expert on human rights law, and I went to talk with the IPTF regional commander.

Bo received a warm welcome from Bowen, who offered all available support and resources for us to continue the investigation. I, however, had a different experience. The Sarajevo regional commander was quick to brush me off, telling me he agreed with Roy's assessment and cautioning that I should not get involved. I tried to present some of the evidence we had collected, but he was not interested in seeing it; conversation closed. I was getting the distinct impression that the DynCorp contractors who were in UN command positions were all going to stick together on this one.

Bo returned to the station with renewed energy, but I was livid. "I have the feeling," I said, "that the shit is about to hit the fan." Bo gave me a confused look. Then a slow smile spread across his face, and he broke into a laugh as if that were one of the funniest things he had ever heard. "Have you ever actually imagined what that might look like?" he asked.

I raised my eyebrows at him. "No."

Bo also cracked up when I used the appropriate terminology for the regional commander: "Major Asshole." He had never heard that one either.

But it was true, the shit was indeed about to hit the fan.

A few days later, Harry requested photocopies of all documents, statements, and notes in the case file of the Hadžići incident to be turned over to the IPTF regional commander.

Bo and I both knew that handing over these documents to anyone outside the UN office of Human Rights who was not involved in the scope of the investigation breached standard operating procedure. This included IPTF officials, unless they had sought proper authorization from the UN Legal Office, which was not the case here. The summons by my DynCorp colleagues was out of order, and Bo and I were quite sure that neither of these gentlemen had taken the time to read the human rights investigative protocols.

Bo immediately reached out to Bowen and faxed over Harry's memo. Minutes later he received a call from the UN chief of human rights office, explicitly stating that no copies of the Hadžići case file were to be handed over to anyone without Bowen's written approval and that Bo should promptly deliver the file to UN Main HQ. Bo hopped in his truck for the quick trip to Sarajevo, where the file was reclassified to fall solely under the auspices of the human rights division. Now there could be no further interruption from the IPTF or DynCorp.

Bo took things one step further: He immediately applied for— and received—a position in the regional human rights office so that he could continue to lead the case investigation.

Back at the Ilidža station, Harry called us into his office, ordering us to surrender the file. "We no longer have the case file," Bo informed him. "It's been delivered to UN Main HQ, chief of human rights."

Harry knew as well as we did that Main HQ outranked both him and the regional commander. Still, Harry said he did not believe us and asked that we leave his office so he could make some phone calls.

Later that week a new schedule was drafted at the Ilidža station; I was not listed as a human rights investigator. With no explanation, I had been temporarily demoted to the night shift at the station and was informed that soon I was to be transferred altogether—to the front lines in Visegrád. I had heard about Visegrád, a Serb-populated area east of Sarajevo that still raged with intense anti-American sentiment. Local television ads and billboards morphed President Bill Clinton's face into Adolf Hitler's, and there had been violent attacks against Americans, to the extent that all U.S. monitors had been pulled from the region. I apparently was to be the first American sent back. To add to my disbelief, there was no human rights office in Visegrád, so I was also being pulled from my area of expertise.

Bo received his papers for redeployment to regional HQ, and soon he was gone. Without him or Jan, I felt alone at the station, eking out my newly assigned night shift, where I pushed paper around a desk and waited to be shipped out to Visegrád.

———

Back at my rented house on Vrelo Bosne, my housemate Weldon casually had let us know that his wife and two preteen sons were midflight on their way to Bosnia and that they would be moving into the house with us. He failed to mention that they were also bringing their big, old, incontinent family dog. Weldon had a single bedroom with only one bed but decided to designate the living room couches as his sons' quarters. The leaky, odorous dog had free roam.

Our landlady, Branca, was furious. Culturally, animals in the house—even dogs and cats—were seen as filthy. This dog bounding about in her home was an extreme indignity, but she needed the rent, so she refrained from kicking Weldon out. My accommodations were now so cramped, noisy, and tense that I had begun to think that transferring to Visegrád might not be so bad after all.

Bo, however, had another plan. He had made a plea to the regional head of human rights on my behalf, and I received a call from Madeleine Rees, head of the UN Office of the High Commissioner on Human Rights (UNOHCHR). I had already encountered some of Madeleine's efforts in the form of a flyer posted around Tito Barracks: "Join the Volunteer Network of UN Advocates Against Sexual Harassment! We are all responsible for confronting sexual harassment, and I believe that harassment and discrimination are perpetuated by inaction and silence." Over the phone, I explained my situation to her. She was quiet for a moment, then asked if I could meet for lunch.

We met at the cafeteria in Tito Barracks. Madeleine brought along another woman, Maureen Kelly, an American DynCorp contractor from Pennsylvania who worked with her in Gender Affairs. At first I was a little uneasy detailing my difficulties with my DynCorp superiors in front of another DynCorp contractor, but Maureen indicated that she too had experienced some of their good-old-boy tactics. It was Madeleine, though, who dominated the conversation. A British attorney with considerable experience in both discrimination law and women's rights nongovernmental organizations (NGOs), she was a fast-thinking, fast-talking, no-nonsense woman who was passionate about her human rights work and unconcerned about whom she befriended or whom she offended. Madeleine was as genuine and straightforward as they come, and I liked her immediately.

"It seems someone does not want you poking around," she said after I had explained the sequence of events. She then gave me a wry smile. "For that reason alone, I think you are a perfect fit for a new joint project we are implementing between the IPTF and UNOHCHR, if you are interested."

"Interested?" I said. "This is why I came on this mission."

Madeleine smiled. "My dear, welcome aboard. You will be transferred to the Zenica station and will be heading up a new UN project called Effectively Addressing Violence Against Women."

The day I received my transfer papers to Visegrád, I also received the papers for the UN position in Zenica. There was no question of where I was to report: In the hierarchy of command, a UN position at main HQ took precedence over a station transfer.

As was standard procedure, my UN transfer document required the signatures of my station commander and the IPTF regional commander. First stop was Harry. He quickly signed, wished me luck, and seemed glad to have me gone from the Ilidža station. I left his office thinking he was simply a cog in the corporate wheel—the DynCorp wheel. Next up was a visit to the regional commander. Upon stepping into his office, it became immediately clear who had been behind the attempt to banish me to the front lines of Visegrád.

"I don't know who you think you are or what you're trying prove," he began, and then mumbled how I was always running around with that blond guy. The blond guy was Bo, and yes, we were running around, busy pursuing this investigation. "Enjoy your time in Visegrád," he said snidely.

"I am sorry you don't like my work," I said politely. "It seems the people at Main Headquarters see it differently." I presented my transfer documents for the UN position in Zenica. Confused, he snatched the papers and scanned them, then reluctantly scribbled his signature before shoving the papers at me and snarling that I should get out of his office.

I would never learn why the regional commander had it in for me, and his mission term ended soon after. He returned to the

States, where he became a town manager. As for the Hadžići case: According to Bo, who headed an eighteen-month investigation, the case brought down the minister of the interior and twenty-nine local police officers, including the minister's nephew, on charges of assault and abuse of authority.

6

ZENICA
(October–December 1999)

Nestled in the river valley, among rolling hills, thick woodland, and snowcapped mountains, Zenica, about 40 miles north of Sarajevo, was the most picturesque industrial town I had ever seen, although it was still reeling from the war. Poverty was rampant as the steel industry was in the tumultuous process of being privatized, and the landscape was marred by profound destruction and looting, which left the town looking as if the war had just happened. Similar sights spanned the country: shell-pocked homes and bombed and burned-out buildings lined most major roads, as if time had frozen them in the midst of falling apart. Shot-down planes, overgrown with weeds, sat decomposing in the middle of fields, and abandoned Serbian tanks were so festooned with vines they seemed a part of the landscape.

I had moved out of the house on Vrelo Bosne in Sarajevo and, with help from the language assistants, found a one-room apartment a couple of miles from the Zenica station, on the second floor of a small block-style house owned and occupied by a Bosniak Muslim family. I did not know at the time that the language assistants often touted residences that belonged to their friends and family (the common attitude of "protect your own kind"), so I initially had been grateful for the introduction to what had been pitched as the best neighborhood, the best landlord, and the best available space in the area. The place was cozy but was butted up against the train tracks, and every night tanks and trains rolled by, rattling my bed. Also, come nightfall, with autumn setting in, the temperature plummeted, and heat generators were not always available or reliable. I was given an electric blanket to use and, while most towns and cities had fairly good service, sporadically the power would shut off, so for added warmth I often fired up the wood-burning stove I used for cooking. I dreaded getting out of bed into the cold and kept my wool socks and boots within arm's reach; barefoot was not an option in Bosnia.

In the mornings, I shivered and hurried my way into the car, where I would blast the heat. But I far preferred the days when I was not assigned a UN car to take home—the Dutch monitors who lived down the street would pick me up (Jan always made sure there were Dutch officers looking out for me) with the windows scraped and the engine all warmed up and would drop me off, door to door.

The IPTF station was in an old steel mill from which anything and everything worthwhile had been pilfered, including the toilet, which had simply been ripped from the wall. The twenty-five staff members made do with what was left—a sewer hole in the floor—as adeptly as possible.

My job was to help implement the pilot project, Effectively Addressing Violence Against Women, A Multi-Disciplinary Approach. The "multi-disciplinary" part meant I would be working with local NGOs, judiciary ministers, judges, the UN, and the local police. I immediately liked the group at the IPTF station, which was made up of about twenty officers and language assistants. The station was very inclusive and made a point of celebrating many national holidays together. At Thanksgiving, I cooked up a turkey dinner; at Ramadan, we took over half a restaurant to join colleagues who were breaking their fast.

———

Soon after my arrival at the station, I received a call from the local hospital that a Muslim woman was being treated for stab wounds and had reported that it was her husband who had beaten and stabbed her. Joined by a language assistant and a few local police officers, we paid a visit to the hospital to interview the victim, whom I will call Azra. When we arrived, Azra cowered in her hospital bed, scared, shaken, and defeated. She begged us not to send her home to her husband.

Through my language assistant, I assured Azra we were there to help her. I took out my steno pad and asked if she would describe what happened. The local police officers seemed shocked—one even balked, chortling under his breath. I looked at this officer across from the hospital bed and pointed to the pad and pen in his shirt pocket. I waited deliberately. Trying to impress me, the officer quickly grabbed his notepad, in his haste dropping his pen. I waited again, making sure he was ready and together, before nodding to Azra to continue.

"My husband stabbed my leg," she began. "I tried to escape from him, and the knife went through my hand. I have told the police again and again of my husband beating me, but, always, they send me back home. There is not much hope now. I will likely die at his hand."

In America, this would have been classified as domestic assault with a deadly weapon—with the perpetrator going to jail and the case going to trial before the state. In Bosnia, however, there was no such concept. Laws regarding assault existed, but they did not apply to domestic disputes. A wife was more or less her husband's property, and spousal abuse was not something that was taken seriously. Battered women had virtually no ability to legally defend themselves.

My team and I learned that Azra had several hospital records documenting past cases of battery. She had also made repeated reports to the Policija about violence from her husband. Each time she was sent home.

"This is clearly a case of felony assault," I instructed my team of local officers, "and we're going to work this case as an assault, regardless of the fact that it is between a man and wife." This approach was groundbreaking.

As soon as Azra was well enough to leave the hospital, we moved her into Medica Zenica, an NGO shelter that offered support and counseling for abused women. Begun during the war, in 1993, by a group of progressive and intelligent women led by businesswoman Duska Andric-Ruzicic, Medica Zenica had an excellent reputation within the community, although it was unfortunately located in a bustling area with little to no security. But it was the best we could do, and it was certainly safer for Azra than returning home. We then began to assemble a case for prosecuting her husband. If we could get a prosecution, it would be the first case of domestic violence tried in Bosnia.

This was no small feat, and we were starting with the very rudiments of police training: how to collect evidence, how to investigate a crime scene, how to interview doctors, how to interview the victim. I thought back to the lessons of my own police training and how the strong and exacting Sergeant Hawkins had influenced and developed my style and character as a cop. "Even though training and tactics will always tell you to watch the suspects' hands," Hawk had instructed, "it's the eyes that are the clincher." Tall and imposing, Hawk had dark eyes that could cut so cleanly through you, it felt like he always knew what you were about to say next. He also had drilled into me a lesson that seemed like nothing more than

annoying paperwork at the time but would become my most valuable resource: "If you want to be a credible cop and investigator,
document, document, document." Hawk had said it so many times
that it started sounding like the popping of a semiautomatic on the
firing range. It was his warning shot and his final follow-up. I would
hear his deep and imposing voice in my head—"Document, document, document"—every time I pulled out my steno pad to take
notes, whether on an otherwise obvious vandalism case or when
I patiently waited hours at the emergency room for a report on a
sexual assault victim.

Hawk was one of the most ethical people I knew, and in a world
of big egos and unchecked power, I was lucky to have come up under
his old-school doctrines. By Hawk's rules, being a cop did not let you
off the hook or give you special privileges; rather, you were held to a
higher standard. It was these lessons I tried to pass along to my team
now. In a country where documents tended to disappear, computers
were nonexistent in Policija stations, and reports were pecked out on
manual typewriters, the basic steps of good police work—gathering
the who, what, when, where, and why—became all the more vital.

I watched as my team of local officers grew increasingly interested in the case and in the procedure. Officers who had started out
with the mind-set that you always believed the man's word over the
woman's were now running through drills of how to treat a rape
victim properly and respectfully. Over the course of working with
them, I continued to impart lessons from my own experience, for
example: In police work, the unexpected was to be expected.

I told them a story from my days as a first-year recruit on the
streets in Lincoln: It was after midnight, prime time for crime, when
a call came out from dispatch: "All units. Rape in progress. Eighty-
year-old female reports white male kicked in door and is now leaving
the area in a small, dark, pickup truck. Suspect is wearing a hooded
sweatshirt." Had I heard the victim's age correctly? I was a few blocks
from the address so I brought my cruiser to a stop, called in my

location, and started to set the perimeter. Then I waited, wondering how this had all gone down. Who the heck rapes an eighty-year-old woman? I scanned the dark, gridlike blocks in front of me, watching for any possible foot traffic. Then, through the trees, I spotted headlights of a vehicle that was driving slowly, as if in no big hurry to leave the area. It could be another cop driving through the perimeter or a drunk on his way home from the bar, but I had a gut feeling, so I turned to be in position to parallel the vehicle and check it out.

A small, red pickup came into view with what appeared to be a single occupant. I called out the license plate to dispatch and advised that I was now close enough to see that the driver was wearing a hooded sweatshirt. He could have at least done himself a favor and taken the hood off. At this point, two other police units met up with me, and we initiated a traffic stop with full lights and sirens. The truck pulled over, and there sat a young man, probably in his twenties. He was calm as could be.

The victim was brought to the scene in order to make a positive identification. I had expected that the poor lady would be beaten up and really shaken, but she arrived clear-headed and adamant. She pointed a finger at the young man and said, "This is the guy, and that's the truck that had circled my house several times." She then gave us a statement that she was forced to perform oral sex on the young man—adding that if she had not already taken out her false teeth for the evening, she would have given him a harder time.

————

Our case file on Azra grew, and after consulting with Madeleine and Maureen at Main HQ, we decided it was time to get the police and investigating judge, whose role was to coordinate a report and submit the case to court for a hearing. Maureen and I scheduled a meeting with the Zenica police chief and his primary detective. This was an unorthodox step; in Bosnia, it was not customary for the high levels of authority to be involved in anything other than major crimes. A woman getting stabbed by her husband was not viewed as significant enough to warrant their attention.

At the meeting, with my language assistant translating, I said, "The police officers and investigators have documented enough facts and collected evidence that will be very credible in front of a judge, and I think we can successfully prosecute."

The police chief and the detective looked at me warily, then the detective spoke in broken English. "That woman is lying. This is private matter of man and wife. She exaggerate her beatings and reports to police."

I pulled the reports—written in Serbo-Croatian, the official language of Bosnia—that my team had gathered and set them before the detective. "That is not true," I said, looking him straight in the eye. Maureen gave me a nervous glance; these men were not accustomed to being challenged by a woman, and she wasn't sure how they would react.

The detective flipped through the reports, then said a few words to the chief in Serbo-Croatian. After nods from them both, we were given the green light to move forward with sending the case to the prosecutor for trial.

I then reached out to a local Croat judge, whom I had met upon my initial tour of Zenica, when I had introduced myself to as many local officials as I could to build rapport and gain support for our special project. This particular judge had inquired about my last name and its distinct Yugoslav origin. Others also had mentioned this, and I enjoyed having a last name that communicated my connection to this region and its people. The judge and I struck up an acquaintanceship, and he made it clear that he was very supportive of our human rights works and this project in particular. He was honored when I asked if he would come to our training site to speak about the type of reporting and evidence gathering needed to successfully prosecute cases of violence against women.

The local officers listened enrapt while the judge spoke, and it was thrilling to see Croats, Serbs, and Muslims in one room, sharing knowledge and working together, knowing that not long ago tensions and corruption on all sides of the law were so great that it was virtually impossible to work toward a singular goal. The local officers were honored that a judge would consider their work effective and valid, and the judge was pleased that the officers were dedicated and eager to serve for the common good.

———

The more I got to know the local officers, the more they began to remind me of my fellow officers back home. Perhaps it was just a touch of homesickness, or perhaps it was simply that cops were cops: No matter what part of the world we were from, we were cut from the same leather. Among the local Policija officers was Monika, a woman in her early twenties with a pageboy haircut. It was uncommon for a woman to be in the Policija, but since men were scarce after the war, equal job opportunities suddenly took on new meaning.

Although Monika was young, she was eager to learn and was extremely efficient with report writing and evidence collection. Her generation had a clear advantage over all others since they had been able to receive a decent education prior to the war. Monika had aspirations to lead the police department in cases against women, and I spent many hours working with her, trying to ensure that she had the tools not only to head up the program in Zenica but also to work on implementing it across the country.

———

The first snow arrived toward the end of November 1999 and turned Zenica into a blanket of white. I had been on the mission for six months now. In honor of every six-month milestone, the UN held medal ceremonies for each contingent. The ceremonies made far more sense for the IPTF from some other countries, since that was their total mission time; but for us Americans, who were contracted for a year, the ceremony was more pomp—and a complimentary buffet. The IPTF commissioner spoke at our ceremony, and we were each awarded a small bar pin with ribbons, which could be affixed on our uniform above the shirt pocket. Most monitors from America and western European countries viewed the pin as more of a souvenir and did not bother wearing it after the ceremony, but the monitors from countries such as Ghana, Pakistan, India, and Senegal really valued this type of ornament and wore it proudly as part of their daily uniform.

———

I could not wait for Christmas—I was flying my three children to Europe, where we would tour London, Paris, and Amsterdam. I only had a week off, so it would be a whirlwind trip. I met them at Schipol Airport near Amsterdam—it was so good to see their faces after six months. Jan was there too, and he gave us a grand tour of his city. I was glad to have the opportunity for everyone to meet, since I was beginning to think that perhaps Jan and I had a shot at making a serious relationship work. The kids and I then said good-bye to Jan and headed to London, where I had secured a hotel with the help of the DynCorp logistics manager back in Sarajevo, John Knight.

Despite the fact that our DynCorp contracts were generated by the subsidiary DynCorp Aerospace Operations LTD out of the United Kingdom, John, British and a former military man, was the only person I had met who was employed by the UK division. (All the other DynCorp employees reported to the Texas headquarters.) John had worked as a DynCorp employee for the past few years, ever since the company had won the Bosnia contract. He oversaw the daily needs of the monitors and kept the DynCorp office stocked with uniforms and equipment, bottled water, and a selection of VHS movies. I always enjoyed my trips to the site office where I would chat with John. When I told him I wanted to take my kids to London and was trying to find an affordable hotel, he made arrangements for us at a hotel that accepted his retired-military status discount.

The hotel was perfectly situated right in the heart of London; however, we discovered the next morning at breakfast that we were the only people there under seventy—it was a lodging for retired military, as in retirement-home–age military. We celebrated Christmas with a goose dinner and the lively music of the grade-school carolers who came to serenade the old veterans.

It was difficult to say good-bye to my kids, knowing I would not be seeing them for another six months. Our usual routine was short on words and long on trying to hide our tears. There was no use being too sentimental. I hugged them all hard and watched until I could no longer see them as they walked down the corridor toward their flight back to Nebraska. Upon returning to Zenica, I launched right back into work to help quell my homesickness.

———

After months of preparation, Azra's case finally went to court in the early spring of 2000. I sat in the courtroom with a few members of the Policija from my team. The case had not been publicized, nor did the locals have much interest, so there were no reporters, no packed courtroom—just a few of us who had been involved from the beginning. At the plaintiff's table, in front of the judge, Azra sat as tall as she could. The defendant's table, where her husband was supposed to be, was empty. We waited for some time, but he never showed. There was no attorney present, either—they were not utilized the way they are in the United States. The judge wound up adjourning the case.

A few weeks later the husband was once again summoned to appear. When we went back to court, he was there: a slight man with dark hair who could not have been more than five foot six. The judge reviewed the evidence submitted, and we were all sent home as he deliberated.

The guilty verdict was delivered in a written finding a few weeks later. I was notified by the prosecutor, and the findings were kept with the courts and police. Although the husband's penalty was lenient—a fine—the win was of symbolic proportions. I immediately called Madeleine in Sarajevo to relay the news. The success of our pilot project rippled throughout the entire human rights community, and Madeleine proudly informed me that she had received congratulatory calls from the UN headquarters in New York. I firmly believed that one reason for our success was that Zenica was more than 40 miles from Sarajevo, far away from the gaggle of IPTF chiefs and commanders and DynCorp officials. We human rights investigators were allowed to work with the locals and make our own decisions—it was progress, not politics, that made justice happen.

The challenge now was to ensure that this would be larger than a single conviction and that Azra's case would become the touchstone for other programs addressing violence against women in the country. This case was a major accomplishment on rudimentary, but essential, levels: The local police now had the tools and protocol to investigate crimes and pursue charges. Officers had gone from making determinations based on hearsay, favoritism, and bribes to having respect and appreciation for enforcing law and serving justice.

Not only did word of Azra's case spread through UN circles; it also traveled throughout the local communities. Suddenly, women, some of whom traveled from the far corners of the country, were showing up at IPTF stations, requesting assistance. Local Zenica police who were part of the project continued to utilize their new-found resources to open investigations, but the tougher cases found their way to me.

The first, in late 1999, was the case of the body of a young woman that was found floating down the river Bosna. She was partially clothed, in a short, tight skirt and revealing top. She had a blunt injury to the back of her head, and was determined to have been dead before ending up in the river. While attending the autopsy I spoke with the coroner, who analyzed her bone structure and deter-mined that she was of Ukrainian heritage. But what no one could answer was how a young Ukrainian woman would wind up dead in a river in Bosnia. A country as devastated and poverty-ridden as this did not see many young immigrants.

The next case to come my way would provide some answers to this first mystery, albeit unsettling ones.

7

AT THE FLORIDA
(January–April 2000)

I watched from the lead-paned window of the IPTF office as a
Policija officer pulled up in a white Yugo squad car and ushered
out a young woman in a skimpy, shiny skirt and tight, sequined
tank top. Her dingy blond hair was matted with leaves and dirt. A
roughed-up prostitute—I hated these cases. In a place as desperate
as this, prostitutes typically were women who had lost their hus-
bands, brothers, and fathers in the war and had no other means of
survival. She listlessly followed the officer as he hurried her inside.

Up close, she looked much younger than I expected, barely older
than a teenager. Her thick makeup was in streaks, and it was difficult to tell the bruising from the puddles of mascara. The officer
spoke to my language assistant, Dragona, saying that the girl had
been found before dawn, deliriously wandering the banks of the
river Bosna.

"He suspects," Dragona translated, "that the woman is of ill
repute."

"A quick study," I said, and Dragona chuckled. "What's her
name?" I asked, but the officer just shrugged and hurried out, clearly
glad to have this responsibility off his hands.

I pulled over a chair for the girl to sit on. She had been brought to me because of my involvement with the program for women and also because no one else seemed to care enough about cases like these to put in the time. I poured a cup of tea from my hot pot and offered it to the girl. She looked up with vacant pale blue eyes, her empty stare finding its way to the American flag patch on my uniform. Her gaze lingered there for a long moment. Warily, she took the cup of tea, and as she sipped I could see her hands shaking. Grabbing an extra sweater I kept at my desk—the building's heat was sporadic, at best—I wrapped it around her shoulders.

"My name is Kathy Bolkovac," I began, making sure to speak in short sentences for the ease of translation. "I am a monitor in the International Police Task Force." I pointed to the IPTF patch on my shoulder. "I'd like to ask you some questions, if that's okay?"

In the expectant silence, her eyes darted from me to Dragona as if she were perplexed. I immediately wondered if she had suffered a head trauma. But her pupils were not dilated and there was no visible evidence of trauma.

"What is your name?" I asked.

"*Kako se zoveš?*" Dragona echoed.

The young woman looked as if she were contemplating the question. Then she spoke. "*Cigareta?*" Her accent was thick and unfamiliar.

Dragona gave me a wary glance as she took a pack of Marlboros from her purse and muttered, "She's definitely not from here," clarifying what I had suspected.

Now, this was strange. With no jobs to be had in Bosnia, there were very few immigrants—unless they were fleeing the war in Kosovo, but based on her appearance and the circumstances in which she was found, that did not seem to be the case here.

I went back to basics. I touched my hand to my chest. "Kathy." Then I pointed to her. "You?" She stared at me coldly, then exhaled smoke into my face. I made sure not to flinch. Patiently, I gave it another go, pointing to the flag emblem on my shoulder. "I'm from America. You?"

She leaned back, crossing her arms tightly. I had seen this behavior pattern before, when I worked on domestic abuse and sexual assault cases back home—her tough, guarded exterior, her way of letting me know she was sizing me up. But here, with cultural differences—and not even knowing where she was from—I was not yet sure, although I did note red marks and bruising on her neck and chest.

I poured her more tea, then poured some for myself and Dragona. We would sit and have tea and wait for as long as it took for her to open up. As the minutes of silence passed, Dragona began to make small talk with me. She and I had become friendly over the time I had been stationed here; she was in her early thirties, a Bosniak of mixed ethnicity who had taken shelter in a refugee camp during the war. She was well educated, her husband was in law school, and she was extremely grateful for this job, which was highly coveted and well paid by Bosnian standards. She had recently had a baby and pulled a picture from her purse of her rosy-cheeked, dark-haired son.

I watched from the corner of my eye as the young woman's face changed while the baby picture was passed back and forth. Her pitched brows receded and her chin began to quiver. She pointed to herself and announced, "Viktorija."

I gave her a warm smile. Now we were getting somewhere.

"Moldova," she said. Dragona excused herself to try to locate a translator, which I knew would mean either bringing someone in from Sarajevo or transferring Viktorija there. Now that Viktorija was talking, she did not want to stop—and I could see that she desperately wanted me to understand. But all I could make out was an English word she kept repeating in her thick accent, drawing it out to three distinct syllables and rolling the "r": "Flor-i-da."

I wracked my brain for some relevance for Florida in Bosnia. An image blipped into my mind: There was a decaying nightclub on the riverbank called the Florida. It was next door to one of the best little restaurants in town where many of us internationals would go for sarma, a dish of stuffed cabbage and various mixtures of meat and spices. I would always see UN trucks in the Florida lot and had assumed it was just overflow parking from the restaurant.

"Yes," I said with an eager nod. "Florida."

And then she did something unexpected. She grabbed my hand and stared into my eyes pleadingly.

I could not wait for a translator to show up; I needed to go check out the Florida. When I phoned the local Policija station to arrange for an officer to join me, I was informed that the detective on duty had not shown up for work, claiming he had been beaten the previous night at the Florida.

As for Viktorija, I was the closest she would come to a crisis counselor or to social services, and I also needed to ensure her physical safety. Our options were few—our warehouse-turned-IPTF station had no holding area, and the only women's shelter, Medica Zenica, was specifically for victims of domestic violence and had no security. Because this case was not clear cut, I could not risk placing Viktorija there, for her own sake and for that of the other residents and staff.

"Make arrangements for Viktorija to be placed in a hotel with an armed Policija guard out front," I told my colleagues.

"No funds, Kathy," came the tired response from my station commander.

I took the beret off my head and tossed in some bills. "Throw in a five, and pass the hat. Sorry, guys, we've got to put her in a hotel for the night." I ignored the groan from my office. I would file the hotel expense, but we all knew we were not likely to see a reimbursement— even though the Human Rights Office procedure encouraged us to arrange accommodations for victims and bill for the expense, it was a ridiculous expectation that a country unable to pay its cops on time would come up with funds for a foreign woman in distress.

————

I set out in my UN truck along with the Policija officer assigned to my station, a Bosniak named Goran, and with Dragona to translate. In broken English, Goran explained that before the war he had been an accountant. "Not many to need for accountancy now," he explained dolefully.

We drove to the outskirts of town and pulled up to the Florida, a crumbling white stucco building with a covered porch, its name partially illuminated by a few working bulbs in a marquee out front. I told Dragona to wait in the car until we had the place scoped out and had formed a perimeter. An "Open" sign was illuminated in the window, but as we walked in, we found the Florida completely empty—no servers, no bartender, no patrons. A few half-full glasses of beer lingered at the bar, and a smoky, sweaty odor hung in the air. Nightclubs with nothing to hide do not clear out this hastily, and it was apparent that someone had alerted them to our arrival.

Cautiously, we moved farther inside. The place was grim. Several tables and wooden chairs, some overturned, surrounded a small, scuffed-up stage. Its centerpiece: a stripper pole bolted to the ceiling. The corner of the room was sectioned off so that a dingy red drape could be drawn around a barstool. Walking around to the back of the bar, I spotted what looked like a metal gun box. I opened it, but there was no gun. To my disbelief, there was thick stack of U.S. dollars. Why would American dollars be exchanging hands here, in this depleted town fortressed by forest and mountains and on the way to nowhere?

As I picked up the stack of bills to estimate the amount, my eyes widened at what sat underneath. There, held together with a rubber band, was a bundle of a dozen passports. I pulled out the top passport and as I opened it my stomach dropped. The photo that stared back was of a round-cheeked, sixteen-year-old girl from Ukraine. I flipped to the next passport: a twenty-year-old from Moldova. And the next: a fifteen-year-old from Romania. And then I opened one to see Viktorija's face, callow and so much fuller than the hollow eyes that had pleaded with me back at the station.

At once, a flashback sent a shiver through me—it was when I first met "Jim from Mississippi" at the DynCorp training week back in Texas. The image of him in swim trunks with his stark white balloon belly, beer in hand as he waded into the pool, came flooding back: "I know where you can get really nice twelve- to fifteen-year-olds," he had said. It was so preposterous at the time that all I could do was store it away, hoping I would not see the day when it actually made sense. Now, as my eyes drifted from the passports back to the U.S. dollars, I realized that today was that day.

I needed some air, so I stepped outside to walk the perimeter of the building. A mountain stream, tumbling in little waterfalls, bordered the property. Under a different lens, this could have been a quaint bed-and-breakfast on a lovely plot of land. But my eye was beginning to recalibrate.

Along the side of the Florida I spotted a rickety fire-escape set of stairs, which led me to a wooden door. I motioned for Goran; protocol called for a joint IPTF-Policija presence on initiating an entry. He sauntered over, and by the look of drudgery on his face, it was clear he would rather I did not follow protocol and just left him alone. At the top of the stairs, he tried the doorknob.

"Locked," he announced with a shrug, content to just turn around. This attitude was rather pervasive among my Bosnian colleagues, and I had spent a lot of time being annoyed by what seemed like plain apathy. Even the country's idiomatic sayings reflected this attitude, such as: "The man who arrives first is not the boss," or, more apropos, "For everything good there will be double the bad." Eventually I came to understand that it was not indifference as much as a dread of what might be found. This was a country of people whose equilibrium had been in constant backflips. Goran had watched neighbor turn suddenly against neighbor. In his mind, nothing good could come from opening that door.

With a sharp rap of my fist against the door, I shouted, "Police, open up!"

Goran shook his head. "Good if you want for us to be shot," he said flatly. I realized this ex-accountant was probably right—not having a search warrant (although we did have probable cause to search) was not at the top on the list of what I needed to worry about in this country. Still, the doorknob did not turn. "No one there," Goran concluded.

But I was not about to give up. It was a wooden door, weather-worn and beaten up, like most things in the country. And so I did my best Magnum P.I. move and kicked it in.

There, on the other side, in a stuffy, attic-like room, huddled seven wide-eyed young women, their terrified faces all too familiar.

"Ahhy," Goran moaned. "Now we have to...how you say...sit on the baby."

The girls were wearing sweat pants and T-shirts that were either too large or too small, their faces coated with smeared, slept-in makeup. The only furnishings in the room were two bare, stained mattresses on the floor, which the seven of them had been sharing. Littered about were a few plastic grocery bags full of mini-skirts and glittery tank tops—their "work" clothes. There was also a trashcan with a wrinkled condom dangling over the edge.

As I took a step into the room, the girls moved closer together, clinging to each other. "It's okay, we are here to help you," I said slowly, enunciating every word. "Please don't be afraid."

I spotted a small notebook lying on the floor, and as I picked it up, one of the girls inched forward, chirping nervously. "Is this yours?" I asked gently.

Immediately, she shrank back, looking timorously to the others. I glanced at the page it was opened to and saw rows of neatly hand-written numbers. One column was for tricks; another was for price charged—ranging from 25 to 100 Deutsche Marks (DM); and a third column was the balance—what she had made, subtracted from what she owed. She owed a whopping 7,000 DM—over $3,000. Her tricks, precisely recorded, one after another after another, hardly made a dent.

"We are going to take you to someplace safe," I said.

They eyed me warily, the same look Viktorija had given me earlier. "Are there any other girls here, at the Florida?" I asked.

Silence.

I tried again. "Are there any other girls hidden? Please tell me, so we can help them too."

A blond, blue-eyed girl pointed out the window, to the gurgling stream below, which tumbled its way into the river Bosna. In a shaky, small voice, in heavily accented English, she said, "We don't want to end up floating."

———

I radioed for a fellow human rights officer to send more cars so we could separate the girls and transport them to the IPTF station. We also needed to coordinate with a local investigating judge, who would gather all the facts and turn a report over to the prosecutor or court judge. If we wanted the best chances of bringing a court case at some point, we needed the investigating judge present for legal testimony to be given as part of evidence. In Bosnia, it was common not only to bring the investigating judge to the scene but to also have the judge present during all victim statements and testimony.

Back at the IPTF station, in front of the judge and via a translator, Viktorija described how her captor at the Florida had beaten her, grabbing her by the neck. He had also threatened to kill a local Policija detective.

"Ask her to describe this detective," I instructed the translator.

Viktorija crinkled her nose and dabbed at her cheeks.

"Pockmarked," the translator said. "A big man. He would come by and drink. On occasion, the owner would sneak money to this detective. But last night, the owner was not present when the detective arrived. The detective took liberties with Viktorija and other girls. For free. When the captor returned, he was mad at the detective for this and held a gun to his head, then threw him into the cellar. Then the captor took his rage out on Viktorija, and she feared for her life. When the captor went into the cellar, Viktorija escaped."

I knew this Policija detective—he was the one who had given me pushback when I had moved to prosecute Azra's case.

The other girls from the Florida were more hesitant to talk. They provided only vague descriptions of IPTF officers, local police, and military men visiting the bar, and it was unclear if they were confusing one uniform with another and what exactly had transpired. What was clear, however, was that they had been scared into submission. Despite their inconclusive responses, my mind kept circling back to the shocking evidence of the U.S. dollars in the metal box behind the bar. The only place to receive U.S. dollars in Bosnia was on American military bases, which were also where we DynCorp staff could cash our checks. All other IPTF monitors were paid in DM, and the local Bosnian currency was the Konvertible Mark (KM). There was something very wrong here.

The use of overseas brothels by soldiers, sailors, travelers—for the sake of argument, let us just say men—is not new or surprising. But the situation here was different. If men were paying for sex with trafficking victims who were being kept against their will and who were underage, then this was not just an illegal visit to a prostitute; this was not just underage sex; this was rape.

None of these young women, including Viktorija, were willing to testify against bar owners for fear of reprisals—and it was difficult to blame them. If I were a young woman whose passport had been confiscated and who had been held captive in another country, I would not want to stick around a minute longer than I had to.

That evening, a convoy of four vehicles driven by local police and IPTF officers careened over the mountainous roads to deliver the women to Sarajevo, where they would be placed in safe houses and repatriated to their home countries by the International Organization of Migration (IOM). I stayed behind, frantically faxing copies of passports and filling out the procedural paperwork for Main HQ and for the IOM.

I felt a twinge of guilt for not going along, but my role in the case was soon to be complete, and I had to trust they would arrive safely in Sarajevo.

A Zenica police officer who worked on the case told me that the owner of the Florida was arrested soon after, but not for holding women captive or for human trafficking; rather, for employing illegals without proper work permits. As for the pockmarked detective who had been beaten up at the Florida, he admitted to taking money in exchange for warning the bar owner of Policija actions (apparently, having free access to the girls was also a perk) and pleaded that his wife had a "disease of her organs" and that she needed expensive medication. He was decertified as a police officer.

———

After the incident with Viktorija, I began patrolling the areas around the SFOR military base camps. Ostensibly, I had already been patrolling these areas, as I always kept a keen eye out whenever I visited the base camps for gas, to use the gym, or to go to the PX. But now very profitable business: Girls and women were herded in, forced to strip, and were evaluated by bidders who bought and sold them like cattle.[1]

No, it was no coincidence at all.

———

In April 2000, as I was winding up my yearlong mission, Madeleine Rees asked if I would be interested in taking over the position of gender officer at UN Main HQ in Sarajevo. (This had been DynCorp monitor Maureen Kelly's job, but her contract was also ending.) The position would be to coordinate training and investigations in human rights cases that involved gender issues, including sexual assault, domestic violence, and human trafficking. I would also speak on the success of our Zenica pilot program at conferences throughout Europe, and attempt to implement the program mission-wide. While this sounded like something I should immediately accept, it would mean I would need to apply for a six-month extension of my contract with DynCorp.

My plan had been to return to the States in June, when my mission would officially end, and apply for a lateral police transfer to Colorado Springs. I had reasoned that after my overseas adventure, I should settle and grow roots in a place where I could see myself retiring, and Colorado Springs, with mountain sports and white-water rafting, fit the bill. Also, I was approaching my fortieth birthday, and there was an unwritten rule in law enforcement that after age forty, the chances of being hired by a new force plummet. So while this new assignment at UN HQ sounded great and would present many new and interesting opportunities, by accepting it I would simultaneously be limiting my opportunities back home.

There was the other pleasant complication in my life: Jan. We had been seeing each other every four to six weeks, and our lives were

I was looking at everything in a different light. Scattered about v
a significant number of cafés, hotels, and bars with names imm(
ately recognizable and memorable to Americans: Marlboro, Harl
Davidson, Crazy Horse, Atlanta, even Hooters, and more than c
Florida. I pulled over to ask some locals how long a particular ca
such as the Las Vegas, had been there.

"Just after the soldiers came," was the response.

On its face, the implication was obvious. In the following weeks
it was as if word had spread through the hills that there were peo
ple in the valley below who would listen. Women and girls began
to show up at the station door. At first, it was one or two young
women a week; soon it multiplied into dozens. Their stories were
eerily similar, and their accounts of just who was paying to use them
were becoming more and more detailed. A clear, but horrific, picture was forming.

This sudden influx of trafficking cases was no coincidence. Bosnia
fit the bill for a healthy breeding ground. Human trafficking follows
a predictable path of infestation: It seeks out environments that are
warm with tumult, such as the aftermath of war or the fall of communism. Then it preys on desperate victims who are brought in over
porous borders and past bribable guards. Strategically, it breeds
near a region teeming with internationals, because they are the ones
who have the money to feed it. All across the country, brothels mas-
querading as cafés, bars, and hotels had sprouted practically overnight around the vicinity of the military bases, where there were
not just soldiers but hundreds of DynCorp employees—mechanics,
food services staff, consultants, maintenance staff, engineers, even
weather reporters—who were not confined to bases. A free trade
market—which, ironically, had been started by an American UN
general who had cleared the land, named the arena the Arizona
Market, and watched as Serbs, Croats, and Bosniaks showed up
in droves to trade food and supplies—was soon home to another

becoming entwined. We talked about living together but agreed that I would first return to the States to be with Erin before contemplating a move to the Netherlands. It was not far from my mind, however, that many international organizations I might like to work for were headquartered in The Hague, Netherlands.

Needing a weekend to think about what to do, I traveled to Amsterdam to visit Jan and talk it over. He was biased, of course, wanting me to stay in Europe. "After forty," I explained to my slightly younger boyfriend, "the eyesight starts to fail, arthritis from old sports injuries sets in. It's now or never for the police force."

"I pick never," Jan said. "Kathy, you shouldn't underestimate an international career, you've really enjoyed the type of work you did in Zenica." He was right, I did like the human rights work, I loved to travel, I enjoyed meeting UN people from all over the world. Colorado Springs suddenly felt quaint and sleepy. More important, my children had done well in my absence this past year, and staying on at this salary would enable me to travel home on break and to fly them to Europe in the summer. And, admittedly, I did not want to be a continent away from Jan.

8

THE GENDER DESK
(April–July 2000)

With Jan's input, as well as my children's, I decided to apply for a mission extension as soon as I was back in Bosnia. I flew back to Sarajevo from the Netherlands, or at least tried to; however, all of us passengers groaned when the pilot announced that he was unable to land in the snowy April conditions and had to reroute the plane to Vienna. Such issues at the Sarajevo airport were not uncommon, and the airport was notoriously ill-equipped to handle weather conditions that would be considered run of the mill in many other countries. There had been incidents when monitors were unable to land back in Sarajevo for days at a time during blizzards, and I hoped this would not be more than a several-hour delay.

I read my magazine, trying to relax—I would call into the station as soon as we arrived in Vienna to let them know I would catch the next available flight out. After we landed, and as I waited to file out of the plane, I spotted the highest-ranking mission official, SRSG Jacques Paul Klein, sitting in first class. Originally from Chicago, Klein was a major general of the U.S. Air Force and went on to become a career member of the Senior Foreign Service of the State Department. He had been selected by UN Secretary-General Boutros Boutros-Ghali to serve as Special Representative of the Secretary-General in Eastern Slavonia, Baranja, and Western Sirmium, and this year he had been selected by UN Secretary General Kofi Annan for Bosnia.[1]

Although I had never officially met Klein, he had spoken at our medal ceremony and was easily recognizable with his coiffed wave of salt-and-pepper hair, his animated face, and his impeccable suits. I probably would have recognized him by his booming voice alone, for he was occupied on his mobile phone, loudly ordering for someone to send a UN plane to pick him up in Vienna.

Once off the plane, I immediately found a pay phone to call into the Zenica station and inform them of my delay. A rapid busy signal indicated the phone lines were down—not uncommon during bad weather. I called Jan in Amsterdam, and he assured me he would keep trying the station and would also fax a notification of my delay that would go through as soon as the phone lines were back up.

I then made my way toward the ticket counter to see about the next available flight. Along the way, I passed SRSG Klein; he had a half-smoked, moist cigar in his hand. Flustered, I momentarily forgot how I should address him and nervously spat out, "Hello, Mr. SRSG!"

He gave me a surprised look. "You're in the mission?"

"Yes, stationed at Zenica. I was heading to the ticket counter to see when the next flight out is."

He grabbed my hand and said that I should stay right here with him and that he was having a private UN plane take us back to Sarajevo. I was flattered and impressed that he would include me on his private flight. Trailing him was his Australian UN colleague Jaque Grinberg, head of Civil Affairs for the mission. Grinberg was the exact opposite of Klein, soft-spoken and easygoing, and we made small talk while Klein boomed to the Austrian Airlines agents that he needed airspace and a landing strip so he could have a pilot and crew come pick him up. The airline staff did not quite know what to make of Klein, and the more questions they asked of him, the louder he became. I glanced at Grinberg, who watched patiently as Klein grew more and more infuriated. Finally, Grinberg approached Klein, gently suggesting that he would make some phone calls to see if he could expedite the matter. Klein agreed and stepped back from the ticket counter and the exasperated airline agents, only to realize that he had just made a spectacle of himself in front of fourteen brand-new mission recruits from Ukraine who had also been on our rerouted flight. Without missing a beat, Klein opened his arms in a welcoming gesture. "All of you who are in the mission headed to Bosnia, come with me."

We all fell in step behind him. The airline offered to make hotel arrangements for us and book us on a flight the next morning. All of us agreed, except Klein. He was dead set on his UN plane coming in and promised that he would get us to Bosnia that night. Either way, we had some time to kill, so Grinberg suggested we wait at the bar and have a beer and schnitzel.

Klein, Grinberg, and I shared a table, but Klein was still immersed in phone calls to Bosnia, which had escalated to the point that he was threatening people's jobs if they did not get a plane to him immediately. Grinberg seemed to ignore it all, asking me where I was working in the mission and what I was doing. I told him about the special project in Zenica, and he was very interested, having heard about it before. When I told him I had not been able to get through to my station commander to report that I would not be on scheduled duty at 1600 hours, he offered me his cell phone so I could continue to try the station. But the lines were still down.

Our group had increased to twenty-five total mission personnel stranded in Vienna. Despite the fact that Klein continued to make call after call, it eventually became clear after a couple of hours that a UN plane was not going to arrive that night. Klein then turned on Grinberg, shouting that he was not about to stay in some dump of a hotel that Austrian Airlines came up with. One of the Ukrainian monitors pulled me aside and whispered, "Who is that man?"

"Head of mission, your big boss." The recruit's face went pale.

I went back over to Grinberg and quietly said that if he and Klein went their own way, I would stay with the new recruits and make sure they made it to the hotel and back to the airport tomorrow morning. Grinberg just smiled and said he preferred to stay with the group. Klein proceeded to cancel our scheduled Austrian Airlines flight (for which we all had paid tickets) for the next morning, assuring us we would all be on his UN plane.

Nevertheless, Austrian Airlines bused us over to a local hotel and put us up for the night. Grinberg rode on the bus, but Klein opted to hail a cab, and I did not see him again until the next morning, when we all gathered at the airport, anticipating boarding the much-talked-about UN plane. We posed for a group picture in the airport—the Ukrainian SFOR in camouflage, the rest of us in casual street clothes, and Klein in a pressed suit, cigar in hand.

We followed Klein onto the tarmac where an old Russian Antonov plane, which looked like it was from World War II, waited. The entry, typically used to load cargo or troops, was at the rear and lowered to the ground. Our commercial flight (which would have incurred no additional expense) was scheduled to leave shortly thereafter. Instead, after snapping another group shot in front of the ancient UN plane, we boarded the machine, complete with bench jump seats and riveted walls that you could see through. I prayed we would make it to Bosnia in one piece. At 1100 hours, the rattletrap managed to land us in Sarajevo, in a field next to a gravel pit, a half mile from the airport.

As we loaded off the plane, two black SUVs, windows darkly tinted, pulled up. Klein and Grinberg hopped in the trucks and were whisked away. The rest of us just stood there looking at each other as the plane taxied off. We picked up our luggage, and I tried to help some new recruits who had a year's worth of gear with them. We started walking in the chilly air.

Trudging into the airport, where it was warm and we could sit, we passed around the few cell phones among us so that we could call rides. I called Bo, and as soon as he could leave the office, he picked me up. I finally got through to the Zenica station, and the station commander confirmed he had received the fax from Jan and was aware of the airport delays anyway, as other monitors trying to fly in or out of Sarajevo had encountered the same situation. He said not to worry, that he had already officially noted that my day-and-a-half absence was due to circumstances beyond my control.

———

Contingents from countries other than the United States did not tend to authorize extensions after their yearlong missions were completed, mainly because their monitors had military or national police jobs waiting for them back home. However, it was not at all uncommon for DynCorp monitors to be approved to stay on. On one hand, an extension, which was doled out in six-month intervals, was beneficial to the mission, since it meant there would be one less person to train and acclimate, one less position that would sit empty until a replacement was assigned and brought up to speed, and one less way to lose momentum—which was a real risk since all the internationals were so transient. On the other hand, DynCorp needed to keep its numbers up, so extensions often were approved whether or not the monitor had produced any positive results during the past year of service. DynCorp was hungry for bodies, and a person on payroll translated to an amount to be billed to the U.S. government, regardless of how effective or ineffective that person was in the field.

I completed the Request for Extension of Tour of Duty form and received written approval from my direct supervisors, one of whom, the Zenica station commander, an American DynCorp monitor, wrote: "I would support an extension of her time in the IPTF mission because of her dedication to the pilot program involving gender issues....She has been a valuable asset to the program and is representing IPTF in a positive manner." It was with a hint of irony that I thought back to earlier in the year, when other DynCorp colleagues had tried to run me out of town and plant me in Visegrád. No matter, now that I had received notice that my extension had come through, I knew I was where I belonged, doing work that was meaningful and seeing actual results. I bade a sad good-bye to the Zenica IPTF staff and to my group of Policija officers. "I want you to know, I really learned a lot, Kathy," Monika said. We all did the typical, unemotional cop good-bye: a firm handshake, a deep look in the eyes, and a swift exit.

The house I had shared on Vrelo Bosne when I first arrived in Bosnia was just a few miles from UN HQ, and it happened to be available again since all of my previous roommates (and children, wife, and incontinent dog) had either received extensions and moved on to other regions or headed back home to the States. This time I rented out the entire first floor, with a large bedroom, sitting area, and private bath. A DynCorp monitor from Texas, Stan, rented the entire top floor. He turned out to be the perfect housemate, as he was quiet and kept to himself.

Branca and her family were thrilled to see me again, and we caught up while sitting on the front porch of their small home behind the main house I rented. I was tinged with guilt that I lived in half their original house, when three generations—six people in all—were squeezed into a one-bedroom cottage, making do with sleeper-sofas for permanent beds. But there were no hard feelings on their side—I was their income, and they always seemed happy to have me. Branca and her mother would leave me care packages of creamy desserts, and if they noticed me dragging in quite late in the evening, which occurred on a pretty regular basis, they would deliver leftovers from their own dinner. I even noticed Branca's mother bringing glasses of milk to the Roma woman who would come begging in the yard with a small baby in her arms. On my days off, Branca would invite me to go along with her, in her little diesel Volkswagen Golf, to visit her extended family on the east side of Sarajevo. I traveled with her a couple of times, and we meandered along the way as she pointed out beautiful parks, the best restaurants, and significant spots during the war. Although she did not dwell on the war, it was very important to her that I understood what it felt like to live in Sarajevo during that time and why it was so vital to keep moving forward. She drove me to a cinder-block foundation, which she said would be the site of her own small clothing boutique one day. I was glad to know that my rent was going to help this family progress and fulfill some of their dreams.

Through my new position with the UN, I was asked to speak at the International Law Enforcement Academy's conference on migrant smuggling, which was to be held in Budapest in July 2000, and I had a week to prepare. Whether it was giving police testimony in court back in the States, speaking to the press, or conducting training programs for any of the number of community programs I had been involved with in Lincoln, I was used to public speaking.

I was honored to have been selected as the UN/IPTF representative, along with another IPTF officer from Iceland, Thor Arnason.

Thor, also based at the Main HQ, was part of an Intelligence Unit called the Joint Task Force. At first, he was reserved, but it did not take long to get him talking about his passion for playing hard rock on the electric guitar. With quiet intelligence and a dry humor, he seemed to always be chuckling under his breath. Despite his expert covert operations training, just the slightest bit of teasing would cause him to blush.

The conference, sponsored by the U.S. Department of State and the International Narcotics and Law Enforcement Affairs and hosted by the U.S. Department of Justice and the Immigration and Naturalization Service, brought together experts from around the world to discuss the current laws used to investigate transnational smuggling, use of intelligence, asset forfeiture, and wire intercepts. The title of my presentation was "Trafficking in Women and Children in Bosnia." When I had completed my presentation, a couple of men from the U.S. Department of Justice came over and asked if they could recruit me. Flattered, I took their cards, but knew I would file them away for later—I was right where I should be, enjoying my work and accomplishing what I had come to Bosnia to do. It was as if all my past experience with policing and forensics had prepared me for this challenge. As Jan had suggested, I was more and more envisioning myself making a career out of this type of international work with the UN.

That night Thor and I attended a reception given by the U.S. ambassador at the ambassador's residence in Budapest. The following night we shared a goulash dinner with American Special Agents, including Agent James Goldman of Miami, who was known for kicking down the door to carry little Elián González off to the boat bound for Cuba.

Several more conferences followed soon after, including one to raise funds for trafficked women in southeast Europe, which was held in Taranto, Italy. Madeleine Rees had asked me to fill in for her there. Little by little we were increasing international public and government awareness about trafficking issues.

Back in Sarajevo, I reported for work at the brand-new UN building, a twenty-story white tower decorated with blue UN flags snapping in the wind and encircled by a high, chain-link fence. It sat on the main road, Boulevard Meše Selimovića, aka Sniper Alley.

I pulled up to the security gates, and an armed guard checked my ID, then waved me into the parking lot, which was filled with rows and rows of white UN trucks: Toyota 4-Runners, Land Rovers, and other three-liter diesels. While there seemed to be plenty of vehicles, there were never quite enough to go around, and people fought constantly about who got to take home a car.

On the first floor was a large cafeteria, staffed by locals and serving regional cuisine: lots of steamed cabbage, potatoes, pickled vegetables, meats, and pastas. There was also a doctor's office, which, as a UN employee, I could utilize. The services provided would be far superior to those of the two DynCorp roving medics, who could take several days just to answer your call. In the basement was a small gym, and outside, just beyond the armed guards at the front security gates, were a couple cafés, where we would gather for drinks after work.

My office was on the twentieth floor with a view of half the city. To the south was the Sarajevo airport, and just beyond that, Butmir— the SFOR military base, where many Americans were stationed. To the west was the building that once housed the daily newspaper *Oslobođenje* (which means "liberation" in Serbo-Croatian), one of the first targets during the war—improbably, this ten-story tower was simultaneously crumbling and still standing, as if it had been paused in the middle of an implosion. Ostensibly the building had been left as a memorial to the journalists who, after losing their offices, printing presses, and nearly their lives, went underground and managed to deliver the daily news, with the motto "Papers from the ashes."

The Gender Desk was staffed by four IPTF investigators and several human rights attorneys—all of us from different countries, including Germany, India, England, Canada, Greece, Austria, and Senegal. We each had areas of expertise, such as housing issues, refugee returns, prison conditions, custody issues, government corruption, assassinations, and my area of gender/sexual offenses, including human trafficking.

It was nice to be back in an urban environment, but along with the international crowd came the DynCorp monitors who had been quickly promoted up the ranks and formed a tight-knit group—some of whom had come from the same police stations back in the United States and had known each other for years. Their behavior, from their attire (untucked shirts, incomplete uniforms) to their slap-on-the-back personalities, was in stark contrast to the more formal, respectful demeanor of the other internationals. One morning, as I stepped into the elevator the chief of IPTF personnel, a DynCorp employee, introduced himself.

"Hey, young lady," he said, even though I was quite sure I was some years older than he, "you're kinda cute." I was not sure how to respond but gave him a halfhearted smile and promptly exited the elevator.

Work was busy and challenging, as more and more trafficking cases poured in, eventually making up more than 40 percent of the entire caseload in the Human Rights Office. Typically I was in the office or out in the field between 0800 and 2000 hours, and my days were long and draining, but I was seeing results. I helped to create "Operating Procedures for Trafficking Victims," a packet to be distributed to all Policija and IPTF stations, providing definitions of a trafficked person and a list of questions to ask when interviewing trafficking victims, such as:

How did you leave your country? From where and through which border points? By which means of transportation?

Were you sold for money?

Were you involved in any sexual acts with paying customers or other persons? If yes, were you forced to do so?

Who used your services (local police/military, politicians, international community)?

Also included was a document for a victim to sign if she wanted to be repatriated to her home country.

Once completed, the packet was to be returned to my office for record keeping and follow-up. These forms provided a standard procedure for assessing and processing victims that all Policija and IPTF could follow, and they ensured that the cases would arrive to me in a consistent and documented way.

I would forward the case to IOM, which would attempt to place the victims in a safe house while the necessary documents were prepared. This process usually took a couple of weeks. During that time we in the Human Rights Office would investigate the possibility of having the victim testify in court against her captors/abusers. It would be a phenomenal act of strength for a young woman not only to agree to talk to the IPTF but to testify on record regarding the identity of her captors and the brothel patrons. So far, no one had volunteered. No matter how much evidence existed, a broken, ineffective system did not adequately provide a safe enough environment or the follow-up care for a victim to feel secure enough to testify.

From the safe house, a victim would be "repatriated," which was a euphemism for swiftly putting her on a plane or train with a little spending cash in her pocket. Once over the border, she would no longer be Bosnia's or the UN's problem. The IOM footed the transportation bill and would send a girl to any country that agreed to issue her a legitimate passport. The victim's destination was typically her hometown, but some girls did not want to return home. Often they were too ashamed to show their faces and knew they would be treated as outcasts. Or their own families had sold them into slavery in the first place.

The sad truth was that after all the paperwork and all the planning, I began to learn that the destination did not much matter. At least a third of the time, the girls did not make it out of the airport in the destination country before they were abducted again. The local mafia, having been alerted to a girl's arrival, would have someone waiting to pick her up—sometimes it would even be the local police, bribed to escort her right back into the arms of the traffickers. In no time, she would be smuggled back into Bosnia to work at another brothel. Very little was efficient in this part of the world, except for the well-greased machine of human trafficking.

———

One day, a case file came in with very detailed and specific allegations: A diplomatic vehicle with a recorded license number was spotted at a nightclub called Moulin Rouge. The person driving the car was an Asian American male, who entered the club and requested several females for sexual services. With clear, identifying factors such as a description of a person and a diplomatic license plate number (which was distinctive and separate from just a UN mission vehicle) the identity of the driver would not have been difficult to determine. Because this case implicated someone within the UN, I forwarded it up the UN chain of command: to SRSG Klein.

After hearing nothing for an entire month, the case file reappeared on my desk. It was slapped with a Post-it note on which someone had scrawled "This was dealt with a month ago!" followed by some initials. I took the file to the Human Rights Office and spoke with my immediate boss, Kaoru Okuizumi. Only a handful of years out of New York University Law School, Kaoru had specialized in human rights law and had spent the prior year working with local judges and lawyers within Bosnia's newly established court system. She lowered her voice and told me she believed those were SRSG Klein's initials and that everyone knew who the suspect was, but the case was being swept under the rug. Kaoru suggested I begin to keep a separate file in my office with copies of cases such as this— she was, apparently, prepared for more cases "such as this." I took her advice and created my own human rights file with assigned case numbers. For each report that had questionable aspects, I would turn over the original copy to the appropriate chain of command, while filing away a photocopy in my office.

Not long after this conversation, Kaoru took a new position to work at the International Criminal Tribunal for the Former Yugoslavia. Transiency was a major problem for the mission and the reason why cases frequently were transferred from one desk to another to another—what often happened around here was, quite literally, "pushing paper." With so many people, so many transfers, so many chains of command, it was far more likely that a case file would be misplaced, rerouted, lost, or even stolen than dealt with effectively. What progress occurred was accomplished painfully slowly. This was the last I heard of this particular case of the diplomat license plates. Although it would have been possible to trace the plate number and have a substantial lead, I was powerless to conduct the necessary follow-up.

9

NO INCIDENTS
(July–August 2000)

"What the hell are you all doing up here at Main HQ in this ivory tower in the sky?" Standing at my desk, red-faced and mid-tirade, was an American colleague, David Lamb. He was the Regional Chief Human Rights Officer in Tuzla, the third-largest city in Bosnia, and I knew him to be extremely conscientious. He was normally very soft-spoken, so his marching into my office and slamming a report on my desk had taken me completely off guard. "One of the local police put his life on the line preparing this report," he shouted, "and nothing has been done for almost a year!"

I stared at the case number that had been assigned by the Tuzla Regional Human Rights Office,[1] hand-written—as they all were—on the file.

"David, I'm sorry, but I've never seen this report before."

He breathed a long sigh, knowing full well we were on the same side. "Take a look," he said. "You'll see why."

The report implicated an American in forging documents and buying a trafficked woman from a Tuzla nightclub called the Istanbul. Also included were names, photos, and videotapes of SFOR and IPTF officers who were frequenting the Istanbul and other nightclubs and paying for services with trafficked women. According to David, it had gone uninvestigated for nearly an entire year. "Hypocrisy," David said, shaking his head. He had joined the mission six months before I had and was now on his second extension. Although he had forwarded the report to the Gender Desk before I had taken the position, proper procedure for any case implicating IPTF was to forward the file up the IPTF ranks, starting first with IPTF Internal Affairs; then, if necessary, to the IPTF commissioner; and then to SRSG Klein.

———

A clear but disturbing picture was forming, layer by layer. The first layer was IPTF Internal Affairs, the initial checkpoint for any file that indicated something was awry with IPTF; at this point, the office consisted of two staff members, both of whom happened to be Americans with DynCorp. Although this was not surprising, given that Americans made up the greatest percentage of IPTF, it did pose an interesting scenario when it came to implicating fellow Americans.

But then there was the next layer: The file would be handed from Internal Affairs to the commissioner's office, where it would fall into the hands of the deputy commissioner. In this position was J. Michael Stiers, an American and the highest-ranking DynCorp monitor in Bosnia. While Deputy Commissioner Stiers worked for the UN, he was still a private contractor, compensated by DynCorp and paid an additional amount for his elevated position. Stiers was privy to all cases involving IPTF, and though these cases were confidential to the UN, it was within the realm of possibility that they were also making their way to the powers that be at DynCorp.

Yet another layer, the most dubious: Deputy Commissioner Stiers, a retired deputy police chief from Aurora, Colorado, hailed from the same police station as the DynCorp site manager, Pascal Budge, who assisted with recruitment of monitors into the mission. Budge was not a contracted monitor on a one- or two-year mission, but a full-time DynCorp employee with a paycheck and benefits and a career that could last as long as DynCorp's government contracts kept coming.

But there was more: If, as has been reported, DynCorp was contracted to receive bonuses from the U.S. government for mission time that saw "no incidents,"[2] this would establish a clear incentive for Budge, the site manager, to encourage Stiers, the deputy commissioner, to deal with any misbehaving Americans quickly and quietly, and under the radar.

DynCorp monitors were American cops, but there was a catch: We IPTF carried a sense of authority that was due to more than our uniforms and badges—we were *immune* from the law. We were not held to U.S. law. We were not held to military regulations. We were not held to the laws of Bosnia.

This confluence of freedom and immunity could make for a precarious situation. I went to work and then had my standing date with John Wayne. But for some of my colleagues, after-hours were a different story. As I watched David Lamb pacing my office, trying to determine what we could do and whom we could trust, it seemed that the test of human nature was laid out as if we were in the midst of a television reality show, where some carefully cast narcissists are locked in a room and the show's producers just sit back and wait for the inevitable fireworks. The IPTF episode was packed with all the essential elements: lots of money; lots of free time to scheme; completely new surroundings a continent away from home; an audience of broken, desperate people ripe to be taken advantage of; corruption plots dangling like carrots; and, the kicker—anything goes, there are no laws.

I turned the report over to the Internal Affairs unit and, as an additional safeguard, I told David we should also give the report to Thor in the Joint Task Force. He would be able to bypass Deputy

Commissioner Stiers and put pressure directly on the IPTF commissioner, Vincent Coeurderoy, a French general.

I don't know who ever did see the file. But no investigation took place, and the accused monitors finished their mission time, collected their pay—including their bonus for completion of a full year of service—and returned home to the United States, where they probably resumed policing and other activities, such as coaching their kids' Little League teams and going to church on Sunday. No one—not the U.S. police, nor the U.S. government, nor a future employer, not even another military contractor—would ever have any way of finding out what they had done.

———

IPTF Deputy Commissioner Stiers had selected a young man from North Carolina, Reid Jones, to be his contingent commander, purportedly responsible for overseeing the general welfare of monitors. Freckle-faced and with braces on his teeth, Jones preferred to introduce himself as Stiers's special assistant, a title we all suspected he had made up. Jones even printed his own business cards with this title and a picture of an American flag rippling in the wind.

The first time I had officially met Jones was in June 2000 at the American contingent medal ceremony, my second one, where we received our pin and a medal for the completion of another six-month term. For many monitors in the mission, this was good-bye—their yearlong commitment was up and they were going home. The rest of us had been approved extensions and would see at least one more medal ceremony while in Bosnia. SRSG Klein made an appearance at the ceremony; as always, he was impeccably dressed in a suit, with no detail undone, including a perfectly pressed pocket square. Each time I had seen him, he had a cigar in hand, and this time was no different. He shook my hand, and we chatted briefly.

Another monitor snapped a picture of us talking, and I later placed it in my album.

The next week I had an email from Reid Jones saying that he had videotaped the medal ceremony, and the tapes were ready to be picked up in his office. I thought it would be a nice souvenir to send home to my children, especially since they enjoyed teasing me about my new fashion trend as a mushroom head from the starchy blue beret. I went down to the first floor to Jones's office. He gave me a big smile and retrieved a copy of the videotape.

I thanked him and turned to leave.

"Are you going to the Fourth of July party at the embassy?" he asked.

A couple of days earlier I had been surprised to receive a formal invitation from the ambassador and his wife requesting my presence at their party. I had wondered how I had been chosen as one of only a dozen monitors to attend.

"Yes," I said, "it sounds great." Then I smiled and left his office.

That night my housemate Stan and I tried to watch the video-tape, only it was nothing but static, so I swung by Jones's office the next morning to get a replacement. Jones looked at the tape. "Let's check this out," he said, and motioned me into the office of his boss, Michael Stiers. It's okay, Jones coaxed, assuring me that Stiers was out of town.

Stiers's secretary, a veteran UN employee, was at her desk outside the office and glared at Jones. But he just ignored her and waved me in.

Hesitantly, I entered, and Jones partially closed the door behind me. He put the tape into a VHS player.

"Are you still going to the embassy party tomorrow night?" he asked.

"Yes."

"What are you going to wear? You know you don't have to wear your uniform."

"I have a black dress I plan to wear."

"Yeah, but—" he pushed, and I'll never forget his next question: "what kind of underwear are you going to wear?"

Without missing a beat I looked at him and said, "Only my best French lingerie, which you will never see. I think I have seen enough, so I will be going now."

Jones looked surprised and quickly ejected the static VHS tape as he called after me, asking if I would like to meet him outside the embassy gate so we could walk into the party together.

This was too much. "I'm not sure what time I'll be arriving," I replied, and left, exchanging a mutual eye-roll with the secretary, who had overheard the entire conversation.

That night I related the event to Stan, who was surprised I had not heard all the rumors about Jones being a womanizer. I had been buried in my work in Zenica, so any rumors floating around Sarajevo were new to me. All I had previously heard was that Jones had been reprimanded by the SRSG for wearing what looked like bars on his collar, giving the false impression that he held rank.

The following evening I arrived purposefully late to the embassy, but Jones found me right away and continued where he had left off, staring at my chest and trying to convince me to leave with him so that we could go to the American military base to watch the fireworks.

I had planned on going to the base but was now having second thoughts. Jones followed me around the party, insisting that we should leave together. Finally I looked him in the eyes and said, "Reid, what exactly is it about me that you find so attractive?"

He gave me a broad smile. "Your nice titties."

For a second, I was stopped cold. Here I was, at a formal gathering at the American embassy; there was no way I would endure this.

"Cut the crap, Reid, and fuck off," I said. He turned bright red, and I pivoted on my heels and left for home.

During the following week, I discussed the incident with several other monitors, asking what I should do. There was no formal mechanism in place to report sexual harassment, let alone stupid cocktail party conversation, and it seemed the only course of action was just to steer clear of Reid Jones.

———

Although significant progress continued to be made in Zenica, I began receiving reports of how other Policija around the country, as well as IPTF monitors who had not received proper training, were handling this pesky trafficking problem: they often arrested the young women who came looking for help or who were found during brothel raids. They tossed these women and girls in jail and charged and fined them for prostitution, not having adequate work licenses, and being in the country without proper identification.

News of these arrests spread like wildfire in the underground community. Most of the trafficking victims who found their way to my office were well aware of the fate that befell others like them. They knew of the fines, the imprisonment, and the risk of retaliation from their captors—they knew, as did I, that young women in tight, sequined clothes, whose facial structure revealed eastern European descent, had been found floating down the river Bosna.

In the midst of this, I did find kindred spirits who were working tirelessly on trafficking issues. One such person was an Irish IPTF monitor, Deirdre Cunniffe, who was the Regional Human Rights Investigator at the Sarajevo West station. A spunky redhead, Deirdre had recently poured herself into the case of a seventeen-year-old girl named Oana, who had been trafficked from Belgrade. A beautiful blue-eyed blonde, Oana was a favorite of her captor, a notorious trafficker who kept several corrupt police officers on the payroll to avoid raids of his bar. Despite the fact that Oana was a drug addict—because her captor used heroin to control his victims—she managed to escape. She made her way to Deirdre, who placed her in a safe house, where she underwent drug rehabilitation. But Oana's captor was not giving up. He wanted her back and cunningly released two of his other trafficked girls to the IPTF as moles to try to find her. He hoped the moles would be placed in the same safe house as Oana and then escape, reporting back with her location. The plan started off well enough, and one of the moles was placed in the same shelter. But Oana recognized her and reported the girl's alliance with their captor. After heavy questioning, the girl broke down, confessed, and was relocated to another safe house.

Bravely, Oana agreed to take the next step and testify against her captor. Her testimony was made possible only because of an unfortunate circumstance: Oana was a girl without a country. She was of Albanian descent and her parents were in Kosovo, but she had no identification or passport for either state. In the midst of great political turmoil, Kosovo would not recognize the Albanian girl as eligible for repatriation, even though her parents were refugees there. Normally, the IOM was required to repatriate a girl as soon as possible, but because we had nowhere to send Oana, she became what, in the United States, would have been a ward of the state. In Bosnia, she was more like a ward of the UN.

Deirdre brought the case to my office, and in discussing the circumstances with the chief of human rights, we decided to take advantage of Oana's time in limbo and petition to set a court date. For the first time in the mission, a trafficking victim was going to receive due process and testify in open court. We finally had the opportunity to set a major legal precedent, and we took this case very seriously. Oana underwent trauma counseling as well as thorough preparation for trial. In the meantime, we also contacted the

American embassy in Bosnia to see if we could find a foster family in the United States for Oana.

One day, while I was working on this case, IPTF Deputy Commissioner Stiers bumped into me in the cafeteria.

"Why are you wasting so much time on these cases?" he asked. "They're just prostitutes, and there's no way any American family is going to open their door to some hooker."

This attitude was exactly why trafficking victims were being arrested and also why trafficking was thriving in the country in the first place. I shot back, "These girls are not prostitutes; they are trafficking victims. There is a huge difference." He just grimaced and took a seat at the far end of the table.

It did not matter what Stiers thought—this was a UN human rights case, and the trial was going through. However, as the trial date approached in the late summer of 2000, I needed to schedule a meeting with Stiers to arrange for special security measures for Oana as she was being transported to and from the courthouse. I walked into Stiers's office, and there sat the notorious minister of the interior, who was in charge of security. (At that point, he was still under investigation for corruption with regard to the Hadžići raid.) Stiers reluctantly introduced me as "one of our monitors" without bothering to mention my name.

I ran through the list of our security needs, and the moment I was done, Stiers muttered, "You're excused." I held my tongue and respectfully left, hoping they would nail down security plans.

On the day of Oana's testimony, I received an urgent call from Main HQ that Deirdre was in need of immediate assistance at the courthouse. I raced over. As I hurried through the marble corridors, I spotted Deirdre trying to shield Oana. I quickly took up the other side, sandwiching Oana between us.

Four thugs associated with her captor had been inside the courthouse waiting for Oana when she and Deirdre first arrived, shouting threats like "Fear for your life!" I could barely contain myself. It had been the IPTF's and the Policija's responsibility to make sure security measures were in place, yet Stiers and the interior minister apparently hadn't followed through with an effective plan, if any.

Deirdre told me that no security measures inside or around the courthouse had been implemented by the local police; no one had been asked for identification; no one had been patted down; no one was arrested for intimidating a witness. Instead, the Policija had just shuffled the goons outside. It was as if they were simply sweeping debris from the room—they might as well have had brooms instead of guns.

The thugs were waiting for Oana after her emotional and draining testimony, forming an intimidating wall outside the courthouse. Again they called her name. One lifted his shirt and pointed to a handgun in his belt. Deirdre and I pushed Oana into a waiting UN truck and got her out of there. I kicked myself for trusting that Stiers would follow through on this important task—I should have contacted the local police myself to arrange the security measures and felt that I had let both Deirdre and Oana down.

Miraculously, by September—and due primarily to the involvement of the American ambassador's wife, Bonnie Miller, who was very interested in human trafficking issues—Oana had been repatriated to a foster family in the United States.

For Stiers and me, there was now a line drawn in the sand. We may have been working for the same company, but we were clearly on opposing sides.

A refugee camp to the west of Sarajevo near the town of Hadžići. Many of the refugees were fleeing the turmoil in neighboring Kosovo. Bosnian Policija guarded the front gate.

View of Sarajevo that I took from the southern hills. The National and University Library of Bosnia and Herzegovina is the domed building in the center. Shelling in 1992 virtually destroyed the entire building.

A former TV station, shot up, along the road between Ilidža and Sarajevo.

I snapped this photo prior to entering the UN flight charted by SRSG Klein to get back to Sarajevo after our commercial flight was canceled. DynCorp used this incident to terminate my employment.

I'm in my winter IPTF uniform and next to me is a Turkish SFOR officer. We're outside the IPTF station in Zenica, which was an old steel mill factory.

At my office in the Ilidža IPTF station in the early weeks of the mission (1999), working on a stack of human rights reports.

With Vincent Couerderoy, IPTF commissioner, in 2000. This was my final
medal ceremony.

An abandoned Serbian tank in the foothills overlooking the city of Sarajevo. This was off a winding road and in the backyard of a local resident. The gun is aimed at the city center.

Although de-mining was taking place throughout the area, mines were still a common hazard, especially in public places that had a lot of foot traffic.

The Sarajevo War Tunnel Museum, which I visited with my daughter Erin during her summer break in 2000. Under the house is the entrance to the "Tunnel of Hope," which was dug by hand and stretched to the airport, enabling life-saving food and medical supplies to be smuggled into Sarajevo during the siege.

Getting to know Jan (left) and my Swedish colleague and friend, Bo, early in my mission, July 1999.

I took this photo of my DynCorp colleagues during the Fourth of July party, 2000, at the U.S. Embassy in Sarajevo. My housemate, Stan Jaynes, is on the right wearing a bola tie, and next to him is soon-to-be IPTF Contingent Commander Jamie Popwell.

10

EDUCATION OF A LIFETIME
(August–September 2000)

T he months were flying by—autumn was approaching, and my six-month mission extension would soon be coming to an end in December 2000. Due to the stress of the job, the IPTF commissioner had placed a two-year limit on continuous mission time. (After serving for two years, a monitor had to return home but could reapply for another year's contract after a six-month break.) I was eligible for one additional, and final, six-month extension. I needed to decide if I should take it.

I had been working closely with Madeleine Rees at the Office of the High Commissioner for Human Rights on trying to reform Bosnia's trafficking and prosecution laws, and I was also assisting with fundraising for a new safe house dedicated to trafficked women and equipped with the necessary security and resources. Right now, the system for housing and rehabilitating trafficked women was inadequate and dangerous—and a prime reason why women were not interested in remaining in Bosnia long enough to testify against their captors. These women were coming to us with serious health problems and, often, drug addictions (captors knew that women kept in an addicted stupor would be compliant to service the clientele).

The IOM was in charge of setting up safe houses and, although they were doing the best they could, it did not take long for traffickers to locate these houses in any community. An alternative to safe houses was hiring elderly local women who would take in these girls in exchange for payment. But the aging hosts were neither properly trained nor equipped to handle the common issues of trafficked women, let alone an unwanted visitor who might show up at the front door. We had already secured a donation of land for the site of the new safe house and had raised approximately 40,000 Deutsche Marks toward its construction. Now we were trying to raise additional funding for medical and psychiatric care and security.

Once the women agreed to testify, we faced the issue of jurisdiction, since the nature of trafficking was that women were moved frequently from location to location, transferred through various underground channels, or bought and sold among traffickers. Many of the women had been violated in several jurisdictions around Bosnia, which made arranging for testimony a challenge since there was no cross-border authority (unlike in the United States, where the FBI can investigate and prosecute crimes in all fifty states). We were working closely with the courts to allow all testimony to be given in Sarajevo rather than having to take the women on dangerous trips back to remote areas of Bosnia.

We were also working closely with local police departments to create an effective system for security and transportation within the capital city. To the women, just being in an IPTF or police station was not enough—they did not know whom they could trust, and rightly so, for they had seen all varieties of uniforms and badges using brothel services and accepting bribes. We were facing similar trust issues—it was extremely difficult for human rights investigators to find reliable and trustworthy local police officers. With no formal means of making background checks, we had to work the old-fashioned way: by building rapport and observing an officer's behavior over time. Although the process was slow, it was effective. We looked at how proactive an officer was when it came to cases with controversial elements—often officers would do the bare minimum or even stall cases in which they feared retaliation. The rare find was the type of officer who had spent significant time undercover to produce the report David Lamb was fighting so hard over.

My head supervisor, Alexander Mayer-Rieckh, formerly a New York college professor who had worked on several previous UN missions and was now the acting chief of the Human Rights Office, was increasingly concerned about IPTF monitors' lack of adherence to the official code of conduct that we all were given during orientation when we first arrived. He wanted to add language specifically addressing trafficking issues and had sent draft documents for me to review in hopes that we could work with Internal Affairs and the IPTF commissioner to establish higher standards and get more stringent guidelines in place.

There were simply too many important and exciting projects going on for me to just pack up and head back to Nebraska. Again, Jan and my kids weighed in. Jan was excited by the progress we were making and believed these experiences would benefit me when it was time to look for permanent employment. My kids also agreed that I should stay, and we made travel arrangements for my youngest, Erin, to come to Bosnia for three weeks during the end of her summer break.

In the meantime, my second Request for Extension form was filled out by my direct superiors. Just before she left, Kaoru Okuizumi, chief of the Human Rights Investigation desk, wrote: "I strongly support this request for extension, without hesitation. Kathy is an invaluable member of the Human Rights Office, and her efforts and enthusiasm are greatly appreciated, particularly due to the serious problems with gender violence and trafficking."

Alexander Mayer-Rieckh wrote: "I fully concur with Kathy's direct supervisor. Kathy's continued presence will be critical to ensure the successful implementation of the . . . trafficking and domestic violence project."

I took the form to the IPTF commissioner, Vincent Coeurderoy, who reviewed and signed it. The last stop for the request was the DynCorp side: On September 6, the IPTF chief of personnel and the DynCorp site manager, Pascal Budge, added their signatures, granting me a final six months on the mission. Mayer-Rieckh sent me an email saying he was relieved that I would be staying on.

———

Every other week, I visited the DynCorp logistics office, manned by a kind-hearted, retired British military officer, John Knight, to pick up my supply of bottled water and hand in my time sheets. I headed to the vault where all supplies—from uniforms and helmets, to Maglites, to liters of water—were stocked on rows of shelves. Stepping inside, I saw three men in dark suits taking DynCorp uniforms from a shelf. One man tucked a handgun into the back of his pants as he reached for a blue shirt with the American flag patch.

I had heard numerous tales that DynCorp was just a cover for covert U.S. government operations; in fact, this was alluded to by DynCorp staff in Fort Worth, Texas, at our training session, and also in a PR video touting DynCorp's "secret work" in Colombia and other parts of the world. The video had the tone of a trailer for the latest James Bond movie, and I had to laugh as I looked around the room at all us aspiring 007s. It was fodder for plenty of lunchtime conversation: Some of us were skeptical, while others thrived on the idea. I was somewhere in between, believing it was not beyond the realm of possibility.

"So," I said to the men in suits, "CIA, FBI, DEA?" The men spun around, taken off guard. "I thought we were an unarmed mission,"

I continued as I grabbed a six-pack of water bottles. They stared at me, unsure what to say, and confirming my feeling that I had walked in on something I was not supposed to have seen. I promptly left the vault and veered to John's desk. "I think I just interrupted something," I whispered to him.

"Oh, yeah, darling..." John said, "I should have had you wait."

One of the men in suits—undoubtedly the best-looking of the three—quickly came out of the supply room to greet me with a wide smile and some small talk, bordering on flirtation. He asked my name, and I could not tell if he was trying to soften me up or gather information or, most likely, both. I knew better than to ask any more questions, although I certainly had some in my mind (maybe they were searching for war criminals?). Besides, the last thing I wanted was for John to get in trouble.

The two other men promptly emerged from the vault and, without so much as a passing glance, they all strode out of John's office. John and I looked at each other, not saying a word. To me, it seemed that if DynCorp really were the front for some clandestine U.S. government or NATO operation that would help to explain why the contractor side seemed disjointed, thrown together, and often inept at managing us civilian officers.

I had more questions than answers, so I picked up a VHS movie, told John I would see him in a couple of weeks, and headed out.

———

At last, Erin arrived for her long-awaited visit. She was sixteen now, the same age as most of the trafficking victims whose reports landed on my desk. I was so proud and thankful that my children understood what I was doing here and that they were willing to give up a big piece of their life with me so I could stay on this mission.

I invited Erin to sit in on a training class I had developed and conducted for new IPTF recruits who wanted to be human rights investigators. Held at the UN building, this class eventually became a
mandatory session for all IPTF human rights officers. As I described
how to interview trafficking victims, I thought Erin's eyes would
pop out of her head at the graphic details of how the young women
are enticed and recruited. Her silence relayed that she was proud of
me yet scared to death.

"I can't imagine myself or my friends being taken and abused like
that," she later told me.

She could not even fathom living in a place where that kind of
thing could happen. I tried to explain how desperate these young
women were for a better life and how bleak their options were in
their own countries. Often these were intelligent women who lacked
a full understanding of what they were getting themselves into—
and often the traffickers were so slick that the operations seemed
like legitimate work-abroad programs, presented well enough to
fool the best of us. Erin shuddered. "Mom, you did the right thing
by coming here to help these people."

My daughter was getting the hard-knocks education of a lifetime.
She was saddened by the number of Roma children begging on the
streets and the sight of so many bombed buildings and "BEWARE
LAND MINES" signs. Although my living conditions were good
by Sarajevo standards, it was a rude awakening for an American
teenager not to have hot water on demand, cable TV, or fast food
restaurants.

We went sightseeing and, most poignantly, visited the Sarajevo
Tunnel, a narrow underground passageway that stretched from the
city center to the airport and had allowed food, medical supplies,
and ammunition to be smuggled in while the city was under siege
and blockaded. Dug by Bosnian volunteers who scraped away at
the earth for six months with nothing more than picks and shovels,

hauling away the debris in wheelbarrows, the tunnel is credited with saving the capital.

The tunnel began underneath a house owned by the Kolar family. (They now run a museum and memorial to the tunnel.) Barely five feet high and precariously braced with beams taken from a nearby fence, the tunnel was a mere half-mile long and had been essential in keeping hundreds of thousands of people alive. Eventually, an oil line was installed in the tunnel to pipe in fuel, as was an electricity cable. The tunnel was also used to transport Bosnia's then president, Alija Izetbegović. Too frail to walk, Izetbegović arrived in a wheelchair and was pushed by eighteen-year-old Edis Kolar to the airport on the other side. Kolar later told BBC News that that was the proudest day of his life.[1]

Erin and I went to dinner one evening in downtown Sarajevo with a German IPTF colleague at a charming old-world style restaurant with white tablecloths, nice china and candles on the tables. We noticed what seemed like security guards posted out front and assumed it was for a diplomat, but as we were seated we realized we were sharing the dining room with former president Izetbegović, whom we had just been hearing about. Only after the fact did it occur to me that I should have immediately turned us around and gone to another restaurant, given the number of attempts on the president's life.

Erin's visit would be my best and most lasting memory of the mission. As much as I wished she could have stayed longer, I would soon be glad that she was not present for the events that were about to unfold.

11

LADIES OF THE EVENING
(October 2000)

Doboj, the oldest city in Bosnia, was built around a stone fortress dating back to the thirteenth century. Loosely translated as "near the battle," Doboj had been captured over the centuries by nearly every empire in Europe—from the Turkish Empire, to the Hungarian, to the Austrian, to the Bosnian. Accurately reconstructed, the stone and wood fortress walls wind up the hilltop, and it is now a tourist destination. Families can dress in medieval garb and take pictures with their heads in a guillotine, or look like Rapunzel with hair hanging out of a cupola window, or pose with a cannon ready to fire through the turrets.

On the outskirts of town, sixteen young women arrived at the local IPTF station during the first week of October. They were originally from Moldova, Ukraine, Romania, Croatia, Bosnia, and Belarus, and had been found after police raided a local bar called the Kent. Most of the women were willing and eager to talk, and they all gave separate, detailed reports of local and international police who frequented the bar as their clients. They described specific identifying features: gold teeth, jewelry, uniforms, tattoos, and first names.

Those of us in the Human Rights Office were always encouraged and hopeful when trafficked women were willing to talk about what they had experienced. This group was the largest and most forthcoming we had encountered yet. We never learned just why these women were so willing to talk—perhaps they had made a pact to testify if they ever got out of captivity, or perhaps it had to do with the human rights officers, how involved they were from the beginning and how effective their interviewing skills were.

The IPTF station commander in Doboj, a monitor from Spain, was especially interested in a particular seventeen-year-old girl. He took her into a private office to conduct an "interview" and was sitting knee to knee with the girl, his hands holding hers, when another monitor walked in. The station commander then tried to persuade the regional human rights investigator that he should personally drive the girl to UN Headquarters in Sarajevo. This drive did not occur, of course, and eventually the girl confessed that she and the station commander had been carrying on a "relationship."[1] The station commander was written up, and the report was submitted to IPTF Internal Affairs—only to be pulled for unexplained reasons.

This was the single largest case implicating IPTF that we had documented yet. I wrote a thorough report of the details collected from the victims and suggested we conduct a photo line-up using computer printouts of IPTF monitors' photo ID badges so that the victims could identify additional suspects.

I made four copies of the report, placing one in my personal files and sealing the other three in separate envelopes. I hand-delivered one envelope to Alexander Mayer-Rieckh, chief of the Human Rights Office; one to the Internal Affairs Office; and the last one to IPTF Commissioner Coeurderoy's office. The commissioner was not in, but his secretary assured me she would give him the envelope. I passed quietly by Deputy Commissioner Stiers's office next door. One of my human rights colleagues had informed me that Stiers continued to berate our efforts, saying things like, "Oh, now we have to be politically correct and call prostitutes 'trafficking victims,'" and referring to human rights workers as a bunch of do-good zealots who thought with their hearts instead of their heads.

I was very interested to see where this case took us. Positive identification of IPTF monitors who were frequenting brothels and paying for services there would send a strong message to mission officials and all IPTF members that these were serious charges. In addition, most of the women wanted to cooperate with the Human Rights Office and testify against their captors and the men who solicited services. The only one to opt out was the seventeen-year-old who had admitted to the relationship with the Spanish IPTF station commander. She did not want to testify against him; she just wanted to go home. Legalities aside, the young woman had decided that the station commander was someone who had been nice to her and who cared about her well-being. In a world where she had been not only abused sexually but also physically restrained and tortured, a kind man (albeit one still illegally paying for her services) seemed like a godsend.

The next morning I turned on my computer to find an email from Contingent Commander Reid Jones. The email was sent to me and approximately 120 others, most of whom were American DynCorp monitors. In it, Jones described—with questionable terminology— that there had been a raid on "some houses of ill repute" and that a "few ladies of the evening" had been taken into custody. He then revealed: "I have been informed that several descriptions were given of 'American IPTF' monitors....Apparently, photo line-ups will be made available to the 'witnesses.'"

My head was spinning. Did an officer just leak confidential information on the particulars of a case—to the suspects in the case? I reread the email. Yes, he did. He might as well have entitled the email "Get your alibis in order, everyone!"

He went on to state that the credibility of these women was in question, as were the "particulars of their employment." Being held captive and forced to work as a sex slave would not exactly fall under the category of employment. I took several deep breaths before hitting reply. I cc'd my human rights bosses, Alexander Mayer-Rieckh and Madeleine Rees, and forced myself to omit the choice language coursing through my mind.

In my email back to Jones I explained that under American and international law, many of these girls were technically being raped when monitors paid brothel owners for time with them. "Since I am personally working on these issues I will bust my butt to make sure any US monitor is repatriated or criminally charged if I can prove their involvement," I wrote. I also made sure to mention that some brothels have hidden cameras and that we had solid evidence.

Not more than a few minutes later, I received a response from Jones in which he continued to berate the victims and question their motives. "In defense of any accused American monitor, I will most certainly attack the credibility of any person knowingly allowing herself to be illegally smuggled into the country," he wrote.

It was my turn again, and I wrote back asking if we could have coffee this week so we could talk about actual cases and numbers. "Obviously you are uninformed on the difference between prostitution and trafficking victims," I wrote. "Prostitutes get paid for their services. Girls do not smuggle themselves into this country, even if they know they are going to work as a prostitute they don't expect their passports to be taken, to be locked up, beaten, starved."

Jones responded that he could not have coffee, as he would be in Paris, "probably in a legitimate place of business." He then went on to insist that most of these women were happy and sarcastically wondered how it was that if the IPTF were indeed "so prevalent in these establishments, then why do the girls not whisper in their ears that there is a problem???"

It was now clear to me that my conversation with one of our top-ranking officials was just going in circles. I went to talk with the chief of the Human Rights Office, Mayer-Rieckh, who was as appalled and disappointed as I was at this imprudent and foolish attitude; he was also disconcerted that my human rights report had somehow swiftly made its way into Jones's hands, violating the code of confidentiality. Jones, the American contingent commander, had no authority to view this report without prior written approval from Mayer-Rieckh or from someone in the Human Rights Legal Office. Mayer-Rieckh said he would speak to Jones's superior, Deputy Commissioner Stiers, but the damage was already done.

The next morning, there was an apologetic email for me from Jones: "What I took as good-natured bantering yesterday, you evidently took seriously." He apologized for offending me and said it had been his responsibility "to reassure officers not yet named that they will receive due process."

Unfortunately, it was never revealed just how Jones got his hands on my report, nor did this apology do anything to curtail the larger issue at hand: Jones was far from the only one on this mission who was misguided and unwilling to try to accurately understand the plight of trafficked women. The irony of Reid Jones referring to his actions as assuring officers "due process" was enough to make me choke. Due process was what my office was trying to act on. Due process were words that got tossed around plenty, but, I would come to learn, when it boiled down to seeing action, there was none—no matter which side you were on.

Still, we had over a dozen victims willing to testify, and IPTF Internal Affairs was now investigating. Internal Affairs had been experiencing staffing issues: The chief of the unit had resigned, reportedly due to a lack of support and transparency from mission officials. Every monitor I knew who worked in this department often felt as if they were just spinning their wheels. One of the investigators on this case, Linda Blake, a Canadian IPTF monitor, was making good progress interviewing several of the trafficking victims, and I was hopeful that because of the overwhelming evidence, this case might see some momentum.

———

I ran into Linda in the hall one afternoon and asked how the investigation was going. She took a deep breath as if she had to prevent herself from exploding.

"There is no investigation," she said. "An IPTF regional commander from Ireland walked into my office a couple of days ago and demanded to see the file on his officers. He then said that there'd been a big misunderstanding in the field, and he had personally handled the situation with the officers and was pulling the investigation."

"On whose authority had he been given permission to pull the file?" I asked.

"I have no idea," she said, "and I can't wait until my time is up in this mission. I can't stand the double-talk. It's like the whole thing is a big joke."

I pressed other human rights investigators in the Doboj region to learn why the case had been pulled and by whom. They all rubbed their temples or shifted nervously and sighed that they could not continue to investigate, they had to consider their careers back home; sorry, but they could not stick their necks out any more than they already had. So now intimidation was not only the tactic captors used with trafficking victims, it was also becoming an effective method used by the high ranks to silence human rights officers in the field.

I could not let this go—the facts were overwhelming: We had a monitor caught, in the IPTF station no less, carrying on an improper relationship with a trafficking victim; we had several first names correlating with specific tattoos and other identifying features of IPTF monitors who were regular customers. We had the evidence to arrest local police officers and IPTF members who were taking bribes from the mafia and raping trafficked women.

Why was I being paid taxpayer dollars to collect evidence that I was then forced to suppress? Why should trafficked women risk their lives coming to the IPTF and giving us information when we were not going to do anything with it?

12

"THINKING WITH OUR HEARTS"
(October 2000)

I was livid that yet another investigation—specifically this one, the largest case yet implicating IPTF—had been stymied. I spent the rest of the day formulating my thoughts and trying to figure out the best way to present what was going on here to mission officials. I was scheduled for a trip home to Nebraska at the end of the week. When I returned in two weeks the case would be all but gone and buried, unless I did something.

That night, October 9, I sent an email to about fifty mission personnel, including SRSG Jacques Paul Klein, with the subject: DO NOT READ THIS IF YOU HAVE A WEAK STOMACH OR GUILTY CONSCIENCE. I looked at this email as my best shot at a forum since every other method I had tried within the scope of my job had fallen on deaf ears. I still subscribed to the view that if I could educate my coworkers about the seriousness of their actions, then the behavior might change.

I began by detailing the seemingly innocent steps a woman takes—answering a newspaper ad for employment as a waitress, nanny, dancer, and, yes, even a prostitute—while being tricked into leaving her hometown and winding up blindfolded and handcuffed and smuggled into Bosnia. I described how captors would confiscate these women's passports, claiming they would be returned only after the women repaid the thousands of dollars spent on travel and room and board. The only means the women had to earn money would be to provide sexual services—and those who could pay the most were the internationals. If the women refused, they were beaten or starved or both. The women were also warned that if they escaped and went to the police, they would be arrested for prostitution and illegal immigration.

I offered up specific details, telling the story of a woman who was forced to dance naked on a table in a bar. For kicks, the bar owner smashed the light bulb above her head and forced her to hold hot electrical wires while she danced. When this began to bore the owner, he yanked her by the hair and raped her. Another account was of a woman who was forced to dance, this time while a man referred to as "the doctor" inserted coins into her vagina.

I wrote:

I wish to express my sincere gratitude to all of you male and female police and civilian staff who have assisted these women in the repatriation program since its inception last year. For those of you who still refer to these women and children as "prostitutes," maybe a simple definition would help.

PROSTITUTE—someone who "willingly" sells her body for sexual services with actual material or financial gain, who is free to quit or leave or say no when they want. (Illegal)

TRAFFICKER—someone who buys, sells, transports, enslaves, entices, promises, kidnaps, deceives, assaults or coerces a person, within or across international, state, county, cantonal, municipal boundaries, or a combination of such, usually organized by more than one person for material gain. (Illegal)

TRAFFICKING VICTIM—most of the women and children "some" of you are referring to as "prostitutes."

It is time we realize this is serious organized crime, making huge amounts of money in this country.

I concluded by talking about my reasons for coming to Bosnia and admitted that while the financial incentive was a big motive, that did not mean I forgot about my main mission of serving and protecting people.

We will leave this mission with money in our pockets, medals on our chests and bars on our collars that we would never have earned in our home countries, departments, or military. Some of us…may have had the opportunity of assisting one or two "prostitutes" get out of a very dangerous and desperate situation.…We may get accused of "THINKING WITH OUR HEARTS INSTEAD OF OUR HEADS," but at least we were able to "THINK."

––––––––

I slept well that night and arrived early to the office the next morning, October 10. Several emails were waiting for me. One was from my Irish IPTF colleague, Deirdre, the chief human rights investigator for the Sarajevo region. "Thank you for having the courage to write this," she wrote. "You are a very professional police officer and I for one am very proud to know you."

Another email was from Don Thomas, the IPTF chief human rights investigator for the Brčko district, which had one of the highest incidences of trafficked women. "This is an excellent, passionate message," he wrote. "I agree with the content and the tone. Thank you for sending it. As you know, we are dealing with a sizable prostitution problem in Brčko District and we have a round table discussion tomorrow with local movers and shakers. I will share the results with you." A police chief from Sycamore, Illinois, Don and his wife, who would stay for long visits, had decided that the mission would be an interesting way to spend a year as new empty-nesters. Don had his work cut out for him, however. Brčko, in the upper northeastern reaches of Bosnia, was still tense with ethnic division; it was also home to the notorious Arizona Market, where black-market trade was thriving—and the most profitable trade was in women. Don and his wife described how it was no secret that some IPTF monitors were cohabiting with very, very young women who clearly were not from Bosnia—these girls, young teenagers, would play outside with the local children and ride bikes in the yard, for they were closer in age to those kids than to the monitors who were keeping them. Don's wife, an English teacher, acutely summed up the scene: "Lotus-Eaters," she called certain DynCorp men, after Homer's *Odyssey*, where Ulysses' men came upon a foreign land and were encouraged by the locals to eat the lovely lotus flower. Eating the plant made them forget all thoughts of home.

Don was instrumental in putting together a report on the status of trafficking and prostitution in his district and the steps needed to combat it. The introduction to the report stated:

> We asked ourselves how we would help the trafficked women and the local police best. The answer we came up with was to give all women who seek assistance, and are considered as trafficked, priority and all the assistance we can provide. However, that would be like an emergency call and will not focus on the real problem. What we want to achieve is a reduction in new recruiting of women to the area, and a reduction in the number of girls and brothels.[1]

Due to direct, combined efforts, the Brčko district began closing nightclubs, revoking business permits of any bars or restaurants showing evidence of prostitution, and arresting those who procured women or engaged in trafficking.

The next response to my email was from IPTF Commissioner Coeurderoy. A French general, Coeurderoy's English was broken, but overall, he seemed to share my sentiments. "I will thank you to recall us what should be the way to work," he wrote. "In any case at our level we try to do something and the work begins with great principles and people like you. Please if you have some time to lose, come and visit me to speak about your sadness to live that. You have not to be desperate or hopeless."

The next email that day was brief and disconcerting—from my supervisor, Alexander Mayer-Rieckh: "Kathy, this was not a good idea. Can we please discuss?"

I reported to Mayer-Reickh immediately. He seemed exhausted. Wearily he said that I should have discussed the message with him before I sent it and that Commissioner Coeurderoy and Deputy Commissioner Stiers were not pleased.

I showed him Coeurderoy's email response, but he just shook his head nervously.

"Stiers wants to meet with you and is saying he wants you repatriated and that the U.S. State Department has become involved."

Stiers had always been negative about human rights work and probably was angry that I had used his own language in quotes: "just prostitutes" and "thinking with your heart instead of your head." Yes, the email was a slap in his face—a slap that was meant to wake him up and shake him into seeing the dire reality of trafficking.

"Will you join me in meeting with Stiers?" I asked Mayer-Rieckh. "Clearly he is not speaking on behalf of the commissioner, let alone the State Department."

Mayer-Reickh declined. "This is out of my hands, Kathy."

Fine, I thought. If he was not going to fight for me I would just have to handle it myself.

I was summoned to Stiers's office that afternoon by his secretary. I had asked the legal representative from Madeleine's office, a Finnish woman named Sirpa Rautio, to accompany me, and she agreed. Having borne the brunt of Stiers's outbursts before, I wanted to have a witness with me, just in case.

As we sat waiting outside of Stiers's office, his secretary turned to me. "I just want you to know all of the secretaries think your email is the bravest thing anyone has ever done in this mission."

The secretaries were typically career UN employees. I forced a smile. After several minutes, Stiers finally called us into his office. I introduced Sirpa, but he paid no attention. "What is this?" he demanded, throwing a sheet of paper at me.

I looked at it and replied, "An email I wrote."

"You have used very bad judgment," he said. "I understand you are scheduled to take a vacation home for a couple of weeks. Well, when you return you won't have your job—for your own benefit. I have convinced the commissioner and the State Department to allow me to deal with this as an American thing. Do you have anything to say for yourself?"

I had plenty to say, but I was not going to engage with him. Just because he was out of control did not mean I was going to start to rage as well. "No," I said flatly.

I stood to leave and Sirpa followed. We walked silently out of his office.

"We need to document this," she said as soon as we were out of earshot, and we promptly wrote down the conversation.

The next day, October 11, I was again contacted by Stiers's secretary, asking if I would come to his office. Surprised, I went right over and found that Stiers's demeanor had changed completely. He was calm and somewhat friendly.

"The commissioner would like to see you in his office. Don't worry, you have nothing to be afraid of. I'll walk you over there."

"I'm certainly not afraid to see the commissioner," I responded, "and I know where his office is." I walked down the hall as Stiers trailed me. At the commissioner's door, his assistant stepped in between Stiers and me, allowing me into the office and closing the door in Stiers's face.

Commissioner Coeurderoy smiled and welcomed me in.

"Why did you not come to see me after my email response to you?" he asked.

He was right, I should have. I should have gone straight to him rather than reporting to his deputy.

"I was informed that you and Mr. Stiers were angry with my email and that Mr. Stiers was going to handle the situation."

He gave me a slow nod, as if to confirm his suspicions. "Are you tired?" he asked. "Do you need a rest?"

So that was the angle Stiers was trying to take this? That I was burned out?

"Well, I am tired, but I certainly am not burned out, and I do not wish to leave my position."

He asked how he could help, and we discussed the possibility of more training on the issue of human trafficking and securing more office staff to help us with all the new cases. He knew I was scheduled for a vacation this week and suggested we meet again when I returned. I left his office feeling relieved that he would stand behind me, regardless of the nonsense Stiers was pushing. Besides, Stiers's mission was ending in three weeks; we would have one week that overlapped at the end of the month, and then we would never have to see each other again.

I returned to my office and told Mayer-Rieckh about the meeting; he too seemed relieved. On October 12, I left for the United States, with a strategically planned one-day layover in Amsterdam so I could see Jan. We tried not to discuss the recent events much, as he felt confident everything would be fine and that there was nothing to worry about.

13

BACKLASH
(November 2000)

I returned to Sarajevo two weeks later, in the first week of November, feeling renewed and looking forward to meeting with Commissioner Coeurderoy to continue our discussion of how the IPTF could better deal with trafficking issues. Instead, I was met in my office by Alexander Mayer-Rieckh, who informed me with regret that the problem had not gone away. Apparently, Deputy Commissioner Stiers wanted to complete his mission time with an act of revenge against me. In my absence, he had been lobbying to have me removed from my position. Then Alexander threw me the curve ball, letting me know that Commissioner Coeurderoy was out of the country, and Stiers was acting commissioner in his place. This was a rather scary thought.

I met with Madeleine Rees, who further confirmed that Stiers had been trying to get the powers that be to rally behind him and have me, at the least, removed from my position. He had even been saying that the State Department was backing his decision and that repatriation was still being considered.

Madeleine, however, had gone to bat for me. She had met with SRSG Klein and his deputy, Julian Harston.

"Klein did not dislike your email," she told me. "In fact, he especially liked the 'We may get accused of thinking with our hearts instead of our heads, but at least we were able to think' part. He certainly did not state he was in favor of having you removed from your position."

I figured this was Stiers's swan song and I would just have to wait it out another week until his mission was over.

————

A few days later, I found a Post-it note from Alexander stuck to my computer screen that Stiers would like to meet with me at 1630 hours. I went to Alexander's office immediately, asking what this was about. He said he did not have any details but reiterated that Stiers wanted me redeployed and that he had heard there was even support from the U.S. Embassy and the State Department to have me repatriated.

"I find this absolutely unbelievable," I said. "Now he claims the U.S. Embassy is involved too? This is a defamation of my character. Just a few weeks ago I received a mission extension with extremely positive comments from all my direct superiors. Shouldn't that suffice to prove him wrong? Does Stiers have any reason for this other than my email?"

Alexander did not respond but cast his eyes toward the floor and seemed near tears. It was obvious to me that he felt he couldn't help.

I called Sirpa and asked her to accompany me to Stiers's office once again. This time Stiers led us to the commissioner's office.

"She can wait outside," Stiers said, motioning to Sirpa.

"I would prefer Sirpa be present during our meeting," I said.

Stiers raised his voice. "She can wait outside and you can talk to her later."

Reluctantly we complied. I entered the office with Stiers, who assumed the absent commissioner's desk and chair. Another man,

Dennis LaDucer, whom I had seen before at the base camp gym, was already seated in the office. Stiers introduced us, saying that Mr. LaDucer had been nominated and selected by DynCorp, the State Department, and the UN to be his replacement as deputy commissioner.

Stiers did the talking; LaDucer silently took notes.

"This is not intended to be purely disciplinary," Stiers began, "and the actions I am taking are for your own benefit, as it appears, or at least as it is taken by the content of your email, that you are psychologically burned out. I've been in the field many years and talked to many psychologists who stated incidents like this were due to burn-out, and the best thing to do is to completely remove the person from the position for a period of time."

He handed me a redeployment form. "This is the commissioner's decision, I'm just the messenger here."[1] I looked at the form, its time stamp indicating it had been typed less than an hour earlier, despite the fact that the commissioner was out of the country. Without the benefit of any sort of psychological evaluation, Stiers was determining that I was unfit to perform my duties and that I was to be reassigned to the Sarajevo region IPTF station, where the regional commander could place me in any position other than human rights.

"I would like clarification on the reason for a redeployment," I said.

"Stress on the job, and for your own good," Stiers said. "The commissioner has the right to place any monitor anywhere he deems fit, anywhere in the mission, with no reason at all."

"Are you going to put something in writing about your diagnosing me as 'psychologically unfit' as to the reason for deploying me?"

"No. This meeting is now over."

I got up to leave and LaDucer followed me out, asking if I would like to speak with him privately about the matter. I looked at Sirpa, waiting for me in the hall, and she and I agreed to follow LaDucer to another office. In his fifties, LaDucer had been deputy sheriff in Orange County, California. "I want you to know I have no history on the situation. This is my first day on the job," he said.

I was not sure why he was telling us this. Why didn't he ask me to give him the history of the situation? After all, he was assuming the position of deputy commissioner, and I still had six months left on my contract. Did he want me to absolve him from any responsibility from here on out?

Sirpa, who had overheard the meeting with Stiers while she was waiting in the hall, began to interject. "Mr. LaDucer, this situation is not being handled according to proper procedures. If a monitor is going to be demoted, the process needs to follow the chain of command and action outlined in mission guidelines. Everything needs to be put in writing, and the monitor needs to be afforded a chance at an appeal. Not to mention there is clearly no reason for disciplinary action against this monitor."

LaDucer's face turned red, and he loudly reiterated that he had no history of the situation. He seemed on the verge of losing his temper, and I realized we were not going to get anywhere arguing with him. He was making it quite clear that he was simply going to toe the line, end of story.

"Sirpa," I said, "let's go."

————

Madeleine Rees, however, was not one to toe the line. Furious when word of my redeployment reached her office, she went to speak with Stiers herself. He said he had years of experience managing police officers, and sometimes it was necessary to move them for their own good, especially if they were burned out. He reiterated that the U.S. Embassy knew about the situation and was waiting to see what he would do, and that the State Department wanted me repatriated immediately.

"I have no reason to believe Kathy is the least bit burnt out, far from it," Madeleine told Stiers. "Frustrated, yes, but that applies to most of us who work on the issue of trafficking."

Madeleine once again went to see SRSG Klein. This time Klein had already been briefed by Stiers, and he simply brushed her off.

"I'm going to stand behind the decision of my deputy commissioner," he said. Madeleine tried to argue, but Klein was not interested and he asked her to leave his office.

She then decided to check out Stiers's story that the American embassy had been involved in this decision. She called the ambassador's office, but no one there had any idea what she was talking about. She was certain that if the State Department had been involved, as Stiers had insisted, the embassy definitely would have known about the circumstances. She followed up by sending the ambassador a copy of my email and including with it supporting documents and statistics.

Madeleine was later shocked when Klein cornered her in the Main HQ and, in front of numerous people, yelled that this was his mission, and that nobody interfered with his mission, and that she was out and staying out.[2] After this, word spread that Klein was dispatching his deputy, Julian Harston, to Geneva to speak with Madeleine's superior, the High Commissioner of Human Rights, in an attempt to have her removed from her position. The human rights world was insular enough that Madeleine was quickly alerted of Klein's move. She put in a call to forewarn and brief her superiors in Geneva; Klein was not successful in removing her from her position.

I, however, was demoted to the position of duty officer and would be leaving the UN building. Bo Andreasson, my Swedish colleague, commiserated with me. "I already knew the American expression of an asshole," he told me, "but you taught me the expression 'major asshole,' and hearing all this has certainly clarified the difference."

———

Over the next few days I wrote my final human rights report, which contained ten cases I had been working on—all involving trafficked women who had reported names, dates, times, identification numbers, and license plates of UN vehicles, and other internationals whom they were forced to service. Hoping these investigations would continue where I had left off, I turned in the report to Alexander, Madeleine's office, and SRSG Klein.

I reported to my new post at Sarajevo West IPTF station. In my new position, I continued at my regular salary of $85,000 to answer the phone, do radio checks, and prepare a daily report of area activities. In the eyes of Stiers and DynCorp, I was as good as banished. A week later, as planned, Stiers left the mission, returning to Colorado. My UN position in the Gender and Trafficking Office would remain vacant for four months. The lack of internal support and investigative analysis began to cripple the work of dedicated human rights investigators in the field.

What neither Stiers nor LaDucer had anticipated was that many of the human rights investigators were still sharing information with me and asking my advice on cases and policy reviews. The UN also periodically requested "permission" from my immediate supervisor for me to attend human rights meetings in the capacity of an "expert advisor." Another aspect that Stiers had overlooked when securing my demotion was that, since I was in charge of the mundane task of compiling all the incident reports into a daily briefing report that I sent to Main HQ, I had access to every incident taking place throughout the entire mission. In fact, I now had access to far more information than I had had at the human rights desk. I knew about every raid. I knew every time a trafficking victim turned up at an IPTF station. I knew when a victim reported IPTF or other diplomat involvement. And I knew from the continually rising number of reports coming in that these problems were escalating out of control.

Not long after I was demoted, I received an email from the IPTF personnel chief—there was an issue with my past leave requests. Apparently, someone had been searching through my time sheets and had come up with six to ten days (the figure varied) in my leave records that were not accounted for, and these days were going to be deducted from my pay. The only leave day that had ever been questioned was the day I—along with SRSG Jacques Klein—was delayed in Vienna due to weather. This had been documented and approved long ago by my station commander as "beyond my control." As for the rest of the days in question, there had to be some mistake. I went to the Personnel office in the UN building and asked to see my file, but was told "someone had taken it." No one in Personnel was able to tell me which specific dates were in question, nor was anyone able or willing to tell me who currently had my personnel file. A DynCorp monitor who was the IPTF personnel chief, said he didn't have the days, but recommended I not fight it, because the higher-ups were already pretty upset and it would only make matters for me worse.

"Oh, I see what this is about," I said. Someone was still deliberately looking for a way to get rid of me. I left the office and went downstairs to the cafeteria. I was sitting alone, eating lunch, when the deputy SRSG, Julian Harston, approached me, lunch tray in hand. Born in Kenya, educated in England, and a career diplomat who had served in UN positions around the world, Harston had a wry British humor, and I always felt a genuine rapport with him. In the hierarchy of the mission, Harston reported directly to Klein. Through Madeleine, I had heard that he had felt bad over my demotion, and I had wondered if he had done anything to intervene. He leaned over me and in a sad, low tone, said it was unfortunate that I had been removed from my human rights position. He wanted to let me know that, in the end, he felt he had to stand by Stiers's decision, due to his respect for the position, although he believed that Stiers had overreacted.

I was not sure how to respond to this attempt to console me. Harston's actions—or lack thereof—had told me everything I needed to know; on top of that, apparently he had been directed by Klein to try to get Madeleine fired.

"Thanks," I replied, not knowing what else to say. I thought perhaps he would join me for lunch, but he just gave me a somber smile and walked out of the cafeteria with his tray, heading back to his office.

14

THE PRIJEDOR RAIDS
(November–December 2000)

I n November, in the town of Prijedor, which was the notorious site
of internment camps during the Bosnian war, an unauthorized
raid of three nightclubs went down. This time IPTF monitors
acted without the required accompaniment of the Policija, rounding
up thirty-four young women trafficked from Russia, Moldova, and
Ukraine.[1]

The women were brought to the Prijedor IPTF station to be interviewed, at which point thugs from one of the raided clubs attempted
to enter the station and intimidate the women. The SFOR (stabilization force) was called in to provide necessary security.

The victims' testimonies indicated that eleven IPTF officers
had frequented the very nightclubs they had just raided. Some of
the men accused were American DynCorp monitors, including
the Prijedor IPTF deputy station commander. The husband of the
owner of the nightclubs, Milorad Milaković, himself a former
Policija officer, called a press conference to allege that the IPTF
deputy station commander had been accepting bribe money—to
the tune of 20,000 Deutsch Marks (more than $13,000). As the

president of the Association of Nightbar Owners of Prijedor, Milaković knew this because he had personally paid the bribes in return for protection from any police action. Fifty-six bar owners and their bodyguards were present at the press conference, and many of them had written on their shirts and jackets: "IPTF Go Home." Milaković described how he eventually felt it burdensome to continue bribing the station commander, so he cut off payment as well as free services with the women. In turn, he believed the deputy station commander and his colleagues decided to get even and raid the clubs.[2]

The conference was covered by the local press, and without evidence of further investigation, the IPTF commissioner sought the resignation of six monitors. The monitors were repatriated nearly as swiftly as the thirty-four victims, who had been loaded on a bus for the five-hour drive to Sarajevo. From there, the women virtually disappeared, flown over the border, where their safety was no longer our mission's concern. Along with them went any hope of testimony and a full picture of what happened, causing the Human Rights Report of 2002 to state: "The events in Prijedor in November 2000 provide one of the clearest examples of [the mission's] failure to investigate allegations involving IPTF monitors in trafficking-related misconduct." SRSG Klein issued a UN press statement that was carried on Republika Srpska Radio, denying allegations that any IPTF monitors were involved in illegal activity and that he had accepted the six monitors' resignations "more [with] sorrow than [with] anger."

"These were our best officers," Klein said. "But they did not follow the rules, and that can not be tolerated. These policemen exceeded the mandate, because they raided the bars without the presence of local police."

But what Klein did not explain was that twenty-five IPTF monitors had taken part in this unauthorized raid. All twenty-five were complicit in breaching protocol. How could Klein have simply selected six to send home? When pressed by Human Rights Watch for more information, Klein brushed off the questioning, saying an investigation was under way. Five months later Human Rights Watch followed up with Klein's deputy, Julian Harston, asking about updates on the investigation and any resulting report. "I haven't seen the report, although I have asked..." Harston said. "It's still foggy. I don't think that there has been much digging."[3]

―――――

The American Contingent celebrated Thanksgiving, 2000, with a turkey dinner at the UN cafeteria. During the meal, the DynCorp site manager, Pascal Budge, along with DynCorp's VP of European Operations, Spencer Wickham, stood up and announced that because of the "embarrassing" repatriations of American monitors, a zero-tolerance policy would go into effect.

I broke into applause—the only person to do so. The room fell silent as everyone turned to stare at me. Both Budge and Wickham seemed put off by my interruption. I wondered just what their zero-tolerance policy entailed—the code of conduct for IPTF monitors already stated clearly that rape or sex crimes were categorized as criminal activity and subject to discipline ranging from dismissal from the mission to, at the secretary-general's discretion, the waiving of immunity, which would ostensibly subject an IPTF officer to prosecution under local law or at home. Granted, local law did not yet have much on the books regarding human trafficking (that is what Madeleine Rees's office was hard at work on establishing), but prostitution was illegal in Bosnia. So far no one in the mission had faced prosecution, and very few monitors had even been officially cited by the mission as having engaged in illegal activities, despite the fact that the Human Rights Office was receiving an increasing number of witness statements directly implicating IPTF.

A couple of weeks later this new policy was put to the test. On a snowy December evening, I was offered a lift home from the IPTF station by a colleague I'll call "Carl." From a small Midwestern town, Carl had been half of a two-man police department. Before that he had spent time in the military, his biceps commemorating this service with tattoos of a bulldog in fatigues and a screaming American eagle. Carl was always friendly and smiling, and spoke with a lot of "by gollys" and "boy oh boys," especially when he described the great time he was having on the mission and how he never in his life thought he would make so much money. His pastime was buying old cars and fixing them up, and he was the proud owner of two ancient BMWs he had bought from locals. Most monitors shared the UN vehicles, but not Carl; he was never without wheels and was always glad to drive the rest of us around. That evening, as he drove me home, he was not his normal, happy self. He told me his girlfriend had left him. I figured he had been trying to maintain a long-distance relationship with a woman back home and she just grew tired of being so far apart. But then he sighed and said, "Yep, she ran away."

I did not understand. "She's a local girl," he explained.

"Did she go back to live with her family?" I asked, still confused, but thinking she was probably a language assistant or secretary who worked in our offices.

"Well, she's not exactly from Bosnia. I think her passport says Romania or Moldova or something...." His voice trailed off, and he looked helpless.

I could not believe what I was hearing. I looked straight at him. "Carl, where did you meet her?"

"At the Como Bar."

My eyes narrowed. "Is it possible she'd been trafficked into Bosnia?"

"Oh, I don't know about that, Kathy," he said dubiously. "I bought her from Tanjo, he's the owner of the Como."

I clutched my armrest, digging in my nails. I knew of Tanjo—he was one of the most notorious traffickers in the region. The Human Rights Office had been after this elusive man for several years—and all the while DynCorp's very own Carl had been having up-close-and-personal dealings with him?

"Tanjo gave her to me for 6,000 Deutsch Marks," Carl continued as if he were talking about a puppy. "I kept her in my apartment, and I wanted to marry her and bring her back to the States. But she ran away yesterday, and she took my mobile phone. I'd at least like my phone back."

I studied his face, hoping this was some kind of sick joke. But his bottom lip was quivering, and he had to bite it to hold back his emotion. I felt like I might throw up.

"Carl, why didn't you go to the police and get this girl out of there legally if you want to help her?"

He shrugged as if that had not occurred to him.

We pulled up to my accommodations and I hurried inside, immediately repeating the whole story to my housemate, Stan. Normally quiet and reserved, Stan said he was tired of me taking all the brunt of these cases and that he would report it himself first thing the next day. Stan was friendly with the interim contingent commander who was had replaced Reid Jones and who was significantly more responsive.

The contingent commander promptly interviewed Carl. Seeing nothing wrong with what he had done, Carl gave a full confession, even adding that he had provided Tanjo with information about upcoming raids. Carl insisted that people around here did these types of things all the time and that all he had wanted was to help the girl, to rescue her.

He was quietly sent back home. Although his name was listed on DynCorp's internal repatriation list—the word "repatriated," ironically, sounded so honorable—Carl was never prosecuted, never fined, never put through psychological counseling. His actions did not leave a mark on his shiny personal record. No future employer would ever know of his illegal activities. So much for DynCorp's new zero-tolerance policy. I spoke to Human Rights Watch about the case, and when a *Washington Post* reporter came sniffing around, the mission's official lip-service answer regarding Carl was that the poor man had been duped. "It's actually a love story," said an anonymous senior UN official. "He fell in love with this girl and bought her freedom."[4]

15

DISTASTE
(December 2000–March 2001)

Throughout the winter, I was biding my time, carefully collecting information, and planning, when I returned home in several months, to pay a visit to my state senator to discuss what was really happening on this mission. Simultaneously, although I did not know it at the time, at the DynCorp hangar on the U.S. Comanche Base Camp in Tuzla, Bosnia, an aircraft mechanic from Texas, Ben Johnston, reported to his superiors at DynCorp that his direct supervisors and fellow employees were purchasing weapons and trafficking girls ages twelve to fifteen from the Serbian mafia.[1] According to Johnston, the DynCorp men would forge passports for the girls, rape them, and, as a pastime, buy and sell them to each other. The DynCorp site supervisor, Johnston's boss, John Hirtz, even videotaped himself having sex with two girls who were clearly saying no and resisting. Hirtz had distributed the tape to the men in the hangar.

Johnston was also vocal about the general lack of expertise of the DynCorp mechanics; their unethical practices of replacing perfectly intact aircraft parts just to pad the government bill; and staff being allowed to work on multimillion-dollar aircraft that carried U.S. military while drunk.

When Johnston's reports fell on deaf ears at DynCorp, he went to the Army Criminal Investigation Division (CID). The Military Police conducted a sting on the DynCorp hangar and, after an in-depth investigation, their findings supported Johnston's allegations. The problem was that the culprits were immune from the law. Although the CID could have explored waiving the immunity of these Department of Defense contractors under the recent Military Extraterritorial Jurisdiction Act of 2000 (an act that had not yet been used to prosecute a single case, despite allegations of offenses), that did not happen.[2] Without citing any solid reasons, the CID turned the case over to DynCorp, which quietly sent Hirtz and one other employee back to the States with no prosecution or blemish on any record. Then DynCorp fired Ben Johnston. The discharge letter, signed by DynCorp, stated that Johnston had "brought discredit to the company and the U.S. Army while working in Tuzla."[3]

———

This was all going on around the same time as my guilty conscience email was circulating throughout the Department of State side of the mission. The higher-ups were likely already in jitters knowing that neither Johnston nor I were afraid to speak up. So they got rid of him and were attempting to do the same with me: Put her on the front lines at Visegrád, take her off human rights, wear on her until she resigns—or scour her time sheets, scour everything, and find any reason to fire her.

On December 18, just weeks after my demotion, the IPTF station commander at my new position, Randall Balch, promoted me with an official document stamped with the UN seal of approval. Balch, who was from Arkansas, liked to reminisce about his Harley and some previous undercover work he had done with the Feds infiltrating a motorcycle gang back home. Hanging on his office wall was a photo of himself on his bike, shaved head wrapped in a bandanna. I went from duty officer to deputy chief of Sarajevo West station/ regional duty officer—the primary difference being a change in my title.

Madeleine Rees also was making good use of my experience— albeit under the radar. She arranged for me to meet with Martina Vandenberg, a recent graduate from Columbia Law School. The previous year Martina had authored a Human Rights Watch Report focusing on crimes against women in Kosovo. She was now working on another Human Rights Watch Report that would be titled: "Trafficking of Women and Girls to Post-Conflict Bosnia & Herzegovina for Forced Prostitution." We arranged to meet at my accommodations on Vrelo Bosne, since we did not want to risk meeting in public. I was surprised by how young Martina was— she had a long ponytail and looked like a college student doing a research paper. As we sat at the kitchen table and discussed the cases I had been working on, she assured me she would keep my name confidential if that was what I wanted. That was not impor- tant to me. Telling the story of what was really going on here, on the ground, was key. If using my name would increase the report's credibility, I was willing to do that. I also gave her David Lamb's contact information as well as that of several others on the mission I thought would be eager to talk with her. Martina and I would remain in touch, and over the years I consistently informed her of everything I felt would be relevant to her research.

———

By this point, SRSG Klein was desperate for a public relations make- over for his mission. "Operation Makro" (Bosnian for "pimp") would be his redemption. On March 2, 2001, at 2000 hours, Klein orchestrated raids on thirty-eight suspected brothels. The next day his office sent a press release to Reuters: "Bosnian Club Raids Set

177 Women Free." Klein was quoted as declaring Operation Makro to be "the most significant action to date against human trafficking and prostitution."[4]

Here was what Klein's press release did not mention, and what was documented by the Joint Task Force, the International Organization of Migration, and the Office of the High Commissioner on Human Rights: Only 13 of the reported 177 women rescued made it to the safe house in Sarajevo; 34 of the "rescued" and "freed" women were arrested, charged, and fined for prostitution and/or not having proper identification. No bar/brothel owners were charged, even though many owners admitted to engaging in trafficking.[5]

The numbers did not add up.

An internal UN report to IPTF Deputy Commissioner LaDucer, written by Adam Williams, deputy chief of the Joint Task Force, on March 8, 2001, critiqued Operation Makro as having numerous operational issues. Williams, a dedicated British monitor, stated: "[I]n a number of cases...the raid was either expected or the officer leading the raid was well known to and 'pally' with the bar owners."[6] Additionally, Williams stressed that the Human Rights Office should have been included in the operation—especially in situations where the brothel owner had been alerted to the raid and had prepared the women to have their passports on their person and to state that they did not want to leave. Williams suggested that his report be forwarded to the Human Rights Office and the regional commanders in order to improve future operations.

The only problem was that there was no one in the Human Rights Office who could directly assist with this type of operation—after four months my position was still vacant.

———

In February 2001 I received some great news from home: Erin called to tell me that her high school basketball team won the district basketball championship and now qualified to compete in the Nebraska State Basketball Championship tournament. This was an honor and an accomplishment for her that I could not miss. Erin suffered from an incurable kidney disorder, and although daily medication helped, she still had numerous side effects, including fatigue, so I knew that for her to achieve this meant she had had to work twice as hard. The only problem was that I did not have any additional annual leave days, since I had used them for my trip to the States over Christmas. My next leave days were not scheduled to accrue until my last month in the mission, in June. When I had arranged for the Christmas visit, I had no idea that Erin's team might make it to the state championships. I knew this would have to be a whirlwind visit, and all I needed was one day of advance leave to have enough time to travel home for the game. I requested permission to be advanced one of these days and wrote a letter describing the reason why and that these unplanned circumstances were simply something I could not, as a mother, miss.

Once my request was approved by the Sarajevo Regional Commander, John Hughes-Jones, a British monitor, I booked my flight. However, the UN Personnel Office at Main HQ returned my leave papers with the note that advanced days off were granted only for "compassion purposes" and that these circumstances were not grave enough. When I inquired further, I was told I should get a doctor's note for my daughter. Thinking that honesty was still the best policy here, I reiterated that while my daughter did have chronic kidney disease, I was not going home because of her medical condition.

The verdict came in: Despite the fact that my station was fully staffed for that day and that I had my regional commander's approval, which was typically all that was needed, I was still not granted the one day of leave. I made the decision that I needed to go anyway. I wrote a detailed letter explaining my attempts to secure the day off and explained that I wanted to be forthright about the circumstances and was aware that I would be docked for this day.

At the game, just like my own mother had done for me, I cheered at the top of my lungs for my daughter. The final buzzer sounded; Erin's team had lost. I watched the girls congratulate the opposing team with tears in my eyes and pride in my heart.

Two weeks after I returned to Bosnia, I received a written warning from Hughes-Jones: "I must remind you that all absences from duty have to be properly authorised....Please be advised that any future breaches of these instructions may constitute serious misconduct and will be dealt with in the appropriate manner." *Fair enough*, I thought. This was my slap on the wrist and, of course, it was not something I would do again.

————————

Still in the dust storm of the Prijedor incident and of the leaked reports of DynCorp monitors' involvement in trafficking, prostitution, and bribery, DynCorp site manager Pascal Budge thought it worthwhile to remind the State Department of our achievements—perhaps the unsavory behavior would be overshadowed that way. On March 30, 2001, he sent an email to all Americans in the mission asking for a description of our professional successes and what impact we thought we were making in order to "help other people understand exactly what it is that we do here." The email made me a laugh at first—who were these "other people"? On many days, I also wondered what exactly it was we did here. Still, I was more than happy to respond. "I usually don't like to blow my own horn, but since you ask..." I began. "I hope you are prepared to accept the good along with some of the most miserable and distasteful things I have experienced in this mission."

I told him about my experience, starting from the beginning, in June 1999, and the various mishaps in trying to get to Bosnia.

Then I described my involvement in human rights investigations and the specific cases that were stymied. I wrote about the September 1999 police raid in Hadžići and how it resulted in the dismissal of twenty-nine local police officers and the minister of the interior—as well as an attempted demotion to Visegrád for me. I explained my work in Zenica, developing and implementing the first Violence Against Women project in the country and how its success resulted in my promotion to oversee all of the gender-related cases in Bosnia, such as rapes, domestic violence, and trafficking of women. I was also up front that I had encountered diplomats, SFOR, and IPTF members who were using sexual services of trafficked women. "[M]any of the monitors in the Mission were completely uneducated in regard to the issue to trafficked women (including American monitors, who were also being named time and time again in reports as users at least of these women)," I wrote. As my conclusion, I described how my attempts at educating colleagues on this issue had led me to be pulled from my position and redeployed in November 2000.

The next day Pascal Budge sent a brief email reply. "Although we might not all have been exposed to the same level of 'distaste' here, I think we would all share in the frustration of the overall experience."

I suspected that my email was not going to make his top ten to present to the "other people" who wanted to know what we were doing in Bosnia. However, I had copied some of my human rights colleagues, and they had forwarded my email, so on March 31 I received several thoughtful responses from monitors in the field. A female monitor from Sweden wrote: "I am happy that you dared to stand up for your beliefs. Here in Doboj region some of us tried but it only resulted in cover-ups....I have NEVER been so haunted. We have a lot of horrible stories up here."

An American colleague replied: "I agree, since they have no idea what we do, nor have they cared (except that we stay out of their hair)....[S]ome of us came to work, to put our hearts and minds into something we thought worthwhile...some of us left jobs and family as volunteers and some of us deserved more respect from DynCorp and the US Contingent. I really don't know how to feel sometimes about it all. A lot of our Contingent deserves no respect at all (I frequently claim Canadian citizenship)."

In a misery-loves-company way, it helped to know that I was not the only one who saw what was really going on in Bosnia. But we were all helpless to do anything about it. The Swedish monitor admitted that she had initially wanted to apply for the position of station commander but then thought better of it. It seemed that the hard-working, dedicated people were becoming so frustrated that the only thing to do was wait out their time. I now had less than three months to go in my mission. Or so I thought.

16

TIME SHEETS
(April 2001)

On April 11, 2001, I arrived at the station to find a DynCorp memo on my desk addressed to numerous American monitors, instructing us to make sure our time sheets were up to date. *About time*, I thought, as most monitors were extremely lax about time sheets, sometimes months behind in filling them out. I called John Knight, DynCorp's logistics manager, to make sure he had all of my time sheets, and he assured me that all was fine.

At 1500 hours, my station commander, Randall Balch, told me I needed to report to DynCorp Headquarters at 1530 sharp; he did not know why. I called John back and asked him what was up.

"Just come to the office, darling," he said. I could tell his voice was strained.

"John, why can't you tell me what this is about? Are you okay? What's going on?"

"This is a very serious matter and you need to come immediately." I hung up the phone, feeling uneasy. I told my colleagues something strange was going on and that I had no idea what to expect at DynCorp. Balch looked away, and I sensed that he knew more than he was letting on. I decided to call Madeleine Rees. She was her usual quick-witted self.

"Maybe they finally decided to do something about the trafficking problems and they want to find out what you know," she said.

"Yeah, that must be it!" We both laughed, but I still felt nervous.

I arrived at the DynCorp office to find Jamie Popwell, the new contingent commander (the position previously held by Reid Jones), leaning back in a chair, his feet propped on a desk. From Alabama, Popwell was tall and fit, with a flat-top buzz cut. He made no attempt to move from his reclined position until John Knight walked in, pallid and nervous.

Popwell suggested we go into the next office to talk, and John and I followed.

"Sorry, darling," John said quietly to me.

We sat down in the next office, both men across from me.

"Because Pascal Budge is out of town," John began, referring to the DynCorp site manager, "I've been left in charge of things. Unfortunately..." His voice trailed off as if he wanted to bolt out the back door. Then he took a deep breath and started again. "Unfortunately, DynCorp has learned that you have falsified your time sheets." He cast his eyes down. "Your employment is now terminated. This is effective tomorrow, so you will get paid for today. I am sorry."

Popwell did not miss a beat. "There is no question about the fact that you took advanced leave. They are considering opening an investigation into this."

"I want an investigation," I said. "I want a UN investigation. I did not falsify my time sheets."

"This has nothing to do with violation of UN policies but is a direct violation of the terms of your DynCorp contract," Popwell stated. "I have received approval for you to immediately begin check-out procedures."[1] He slid over a letter of termination, signed by both him and John.

"And here's the evidence," he said, sliding over a copy of the duty roster from the year before. The "evidence" showed the day I was stranded in Vienna and flew back on the UN plane with SRSG Klein. That is what they had on me?

"This is ridiculous," I said. "This day was accounted for as beyond my control."

There was no response. In spite of the fact that I had evidence, including the photo of myself with Klein and the other monitors, to show that I hadn't committed any wrongdoing, they were not about to listen to any reasoning. Their minds were made up. I asked for copies of the paperwork, and Popwell left the room to make them.

John lowered his voice. "I know, darling, I already told them that."

Popwell returned and began making calls to the UN to schedule my appointments for checkout. John then asked me to sign the letter of termination. I refused to do so.

"And knock off the phone calls, Jamie," I said. "I know how to make my own arrangements, and no one's going to kick me out of Bosnia." I left the building.

———

My first call was to Jan in Amsterdam. "Yeah, right, you are joking," he said.

"Well, no I'm not. You know how we had plans to live together; it may be sooner than you think. Do you know a good attorney in Europe?"

Jan suggested I go directly to Madeleine Rees, who was herself a non-practicing attorney, and see if she could refer me to someone. I went straight to Main HQ and watched Madeleine's face drop as I told her.

"Kathy, they cannot just fire you, you have a right to a hearing, and representation. This is just bollocks." We scoured a copy of my contract and noted that even though DynCorp was an American company based in Virginia and Texas, the fine print indicated it was governed under the laws of England. "Quite clearly, DynCorp doesn't like what you've found out about them, and you should fight back." She gave me the number for Bailey Wright & Co., in Birmingham, England. "Call Karen Bailey straightaway. She'll help you."

Next, Madeleine walked me over to the UN House Criminal Justice Advisory Unit, where the chief of the unit, Stephanie McPhail, and I spent the rest of the day preparing a letter of appeal and request for proper investigation and due process:

> I am writing in respect of the meeting... during which I was summarily dismissed by DynCorp ostensibly under section 17 A iv: Termination for cause. I note from the contract that I signed with DynCorp Aerospace Operations (UK) Ltd. that the terms of the contract are governed and interpreted under the laws of England. I am sure that DynCorp are aware, therefore, that there is no provision under English law for summary dismissal without due process. In the event of allegations being made there needs to be a full investigation, which would include interviewing and obtaining evidence from the person under suspicion. If necessary this would be followed by a disciplinary hearing at which time the individual should be accompanied by a representative of choice. Should dismissal be the decided outcome, then there would be a possibility of appeal.

McPhail also advised me to continue to report for work and await further outcomes.

That evening I bought myself a small tape recorder, the kind I used to carry with me when I conducted traffic stops back in

Lincoln—as a cop on solo duty, you never knew what craziness you might encounter, and a pocket recorder was a witness that always held up in court. Now I hoped the same would be true.

The next day, accompanied by a Canadian colleague, Rosario Ioanna, I delivered a copy of my letter of appeal to the IPTF commissioner's office. The commissioner was not in but I spoke with his secretary, requesting to set up a meeting. Next was SRSG Klein's office. He was not in either, but his secretary informed me that his next available appointment that day was at 1615 hours and that I should come back then. I left my letter of appeal, and as I was leaving the office I bumped into the UN head of Civil Affairs, Jaque Grinberg. We greeted each other and I lightheartedly asked if he remembered our Vienna layover.

He laughed and joked that those were some of his fondest memories.

"Mine too," I said. "Especially since I was fired over it yesterday."

Grinberg looked shocked. "No prior warning?" he asked.

"Absolutely none."

One of the secretaries called out, "You didn't sign anything, did you?"

"No."

"Good," she said. "We can still help you."

Grinberg gave me a nod and now seemed in a hurry to be on his way. The secretary assured me they could get some assistance going and that we would talk further when I reported back later for my meeting with Klein. Encouraged, I continued on to deliver the rest of my letters, Rosario by my side. I spotted Jamie Popwell in the cafeteria and walked up to him. He seemed surprised to see me, having assumed I had been in the process of checking out and heading back to the States. I silently placed a copy of the letter in front of him and walked away.

As Rosario and I waited for the elevator, Popwell came charging around the corner like a raging bull, yelling that he needed to talk with me in his office immediately.

"No you don't," I began, surreptitiously reaching into my pocket to click on the tape recorder. "Anything you say should be said to my attorney."

By this time others had gathered around, waiting for the elevator, but that did not stop Popwell. He clenched his teeth and shook his fist at me, then he stepped within inches of my face. I could see Rosario twitching, but he was too small to take Popwell. I straightened up, trying not to wince as Popwell spat his words at me:

"I'm gonna tell you this in front of him and everybody else, when you come back...you're not gonna have a UN ID, you're not gonna have a UN job, you do not have a job with the Department of State. The Department of State holds your contract, they are the ones who are pulling your contract, you don't have a right to appeal, you don't have a right to a dismissal hearing or anything. Do you understand?"

No, I did not understand, but I did not need to explain anything further to Jamie Popwell or anyone from DynCorp. "Thank you, Jamie," was all I could think to say. I prayed my tape recorder was running.

He continued, "So when you come back...if you come back, you are not gonna be allowed, you're not gonna be allowed in the UN building, you're not gonna be allowed on any UN property. Do you understand?"

"Thank you, Jamie."

"You are not being paid."

"Thank you, Jamie."

His face was bright red. "You're welcome."

After the scene at the elevator, Rosario and I went with to his office, where we closed the door and looked at each other with disbelief over what had just happened.

"What the heck was that?" I asked.

Rosario shrugged, speechless. Then we both started laughing and shaking our heads. Rosario then turned serious, saying he wanted to confide in me about what was happening or, more important, not happening with a case he was working. The case contained evidence of organized crime members within the ranks of the IPTF—and human rights investigators were being threatened to halt further investigations.

The case had been handed over to IPTF Internal Affairs by my human rights colleague David Lamb, who had collected more than enough evidence to justify a criminal investigation: Two Romanian IPTF officers had allegedly recruited Romanian women, purchased false work papers for them, and sold them into Bosnian brothels. Lamb and his team had received numerous threats, including from one of the suspects: "Stop immediately anything against Romanians, and do not mess with me, neither with my colleague....I'll not tell you more, but I think you can guess what can happen." In addition, the UN's Ukrainian police chief of staff had ordered investigators to overlook the activity of the Romanians and instead to focus on the sexual misconduct of officers from Fiji and Pakistan.

Despite the evidence, the case languished. "[T]here were credible witnesses, but I found a real reluctance on the part of the United Nations...leadership to investigate these allegations," Lamb would tell reporter Colum Lynch several months later for a December 27, 2001, *Washington Post* article, headlined: "U.N. Halted Probe of Officers' Alleged Role in Sex Trafficking; Lack of Support from Above, in Field Impeded Investigators."[2] When Lamb's mission time had ended, the case was forwarded to Rosario in internal affairs. Now it was Rosario's turn to be disgusted, and he relayed to me how several Romanian IPTF monitors had tried to further impede his investigations by kidnapping victims from police custody and intimidating other witnesses. I nodded as Rosario talked—yes, something needed to be done.

I returned to Klein's office that afternoon for my scheduled appointment, and the atmosphere had changed. The secretaries who earlier had been brazen and talkative now were reticent. Klein's secretary looked at me and said somberly, "I gave Mr. Klein your message, and he is going to turn this over to the chief of civilian personnel—"

We were interrupted by yelling coming from behind Klein's office door. Eager to get me out of earshot, she ushered me to the personnel chief's office, where she introduced me to his secretary, saying an appointment had been scheduled for me. The women exchanged nervous glances.

The personnel chief's secretary said, "Okay...you know he is in there with Klein right now."

"Well, can you just seat Ms. Bolkovac in the other office?" Klein's secretary asked.

It was obvious that they were running out of ways to cover for their bosses. "It's okay, ladies," I interrupted, letting them off the hook. "Clearly, Klein doesn't want to meet with me and is passing the buck. I'll just be on my way."

They gave me empathetic glances as I turned to leave.

When I went to visit the DynCorp office to give Logistics Manager John Knight a copy of my appeal letter, I made sure my tape recorder was running.

"Listen, darling, I need to talk to you personally, and this is between you and me," John said. "I know what you are after, but the best way to go about this is actually to go...go on back to the States."

"So basically you are saying that DynCorp is not held accountable to any kind of labor laws and the State Department is not held by labor law?" I asked.

"That's for DynCorp in Fort Worth and you to deal with."

"Well, you know, John, the UN had had no official notice from anybody at DynCorp that I have been repatriated."

"Jamie should be involved with the UN..."

I scoffed. "Popwell hasn't even been able to produce documentation for all alleged fraudulent dates on the time sheets. You know how many problems we have had with time sheets—I mean, monitors go for months and don't bother to fill them out."

John nodded in agreement. He began to read my appeal letter and chuckled under his breath. "You know, you are dead right in what you are saying here about the laws of England. I mean, I have tried to point that out to DynCorp on a number of occasions, but I mean DynCorp has taken legal advice on how to word their contracts and I'm not in a position to deal with contracts. I am just the guy who bears the contract...I am just the man in the middle."

"John, in the record it says that on more than one occasion I falsified time sheets. You did not mention this or give me any documentation on this."

"Yes, on the evidence of the contingent commander; he handed over papers."

"He didn't hand anything over to me."

"He was supposed to give you all of the copies, there was supposed to be seven days of MSA that they were talking about."

"Well, they deducted ten days of MSA....So, is the UN requesting I be fired? No one from the UN has opened up an internal investigation on this matter."

"The decision was made." John sighed. "This decision was made by DynCorp, okay. I had to be in the position to be the man that had to do that, under the evidence that was given me, which is why I have done what I have done."

———

The following day, at 0815 hours, I reported for work at the IPTF station as usual, dressed in my uniform. When Randall Balch, the station commander, saw me, his eyes bulged.

"What are you doing here, Kathy?"

"Reporting for duty," I said.

"Uh...you've been taken off the duty roster," he said. "I had been informed you'd been terminated."

"I haven't accepted the termination without my right for an appeal and am requesting to be placed back on the duty roster."

Balch and I had always been on good terms—he had promoted me, after all—and I knew I was putting him in an awkward position. But I needed to stand firm. I needed to do as the UN legal advisor had instructed and report for work, as would have been my right had DynCorp followed proper procedure.

"Randall, did you get notification from the UN to take me off the duty roster?" I asked, knowing that, at most, he had received a phone call from Jamie Popwell, the American contingent commander. Randall dutifully had me filled back in on the day's roster.

Not many others at the station were fully aware of what was going on; if anything, they had only heard rumors. I smiled and acted like nothing was out of the ordinary. In the meantime, Balch immediately went in his office, closed the door, and, I would soon learn, called Popwell, who jumped into action. Popwell faxed DynCorp's letter stating that I had been terminated with cause to the UN Personnel Office; from there, it was faxed to my regional commander, John Hughes-Jones, whose office was a few doors from mine at the IPTF station. In a way, my day's goal had now been accomplished: My legal team would soon possess, in writing, evidence that both DynCorp and the UN had refused me the right to due process.

Hughes-Jones called me into his office. We had always had a nice rapport, and he was attempting to handle the situation as diplomatically as possible. "Kathy, I've received a message from DynCorp and UN Personnel that I am to collect your UN ID and driver's license."

I nodded. I had made my point, so I complied, handing over my UN-issued ID cards.

Over the next couple of days, dressed in civilian clothes, I went through the check-out procedure, turning in my radio at the UN, my uniform and emergency bag to Logistics, getting my UN vehicle inspected, getting signature after signature from the heads of various departments. Here I was, being fired and kicked out of the mission with no appeal, and yet I still was expected to go like a good little soldier to all these departments or else I would not see my last month's pay.

I was able to schedule a meeting during these last few days in Bosnia with SRSG Klein's deputy chief, Julian Harston. My last contact with him had been when he had made a brief attempt to console me in the cafeteria after I had been demoted a few months earlier; now I hoped he would have a compassionate ear for what was happening. Before the meeting, I put a new tape in my recorder and tested it. But as I approached the UN building, I felt nervous about running it. The recorder was in the side pocket of my jacket, a normal spot for one's keys. I decided to roll it anyway. What was the worst that could happen? I thought. I was already being forced out.

Once I was through the UN gate check and security had verified my appointment, I was pleasantly greeted by Harston in his office. He motioned for me to have a seat, then he got straight to the point, saying that he understood I was having some issues with DynCorp. I began to detail the situation, and he interrupted to say he was willing to listen, although he wanted to make it clear that his hands were tied and that this was between DynCorp and me.

"I'd just like your opinion on a few things then," I said. Harston quickly jumped up and walked toward his desk. At first I thought, *Oh my God, he noticed the recorder.* When I looked down at my lap, I could see its square outline on my thigh and quickly adjusted my jacket. The phone rang, and I nearly leapt out of my chair. Harston answered, muttered a few words, then hung up.

"I'm sorry," he said, "We need to end this meeting as it appears an emergency has come up." He explained there was a reported riot in town that needed to be quelled, but he assured me that he would conduct some further investigations into my case and see what he could do.

Just as I was leaving his office, a formidable group approached: IPTF Commissioner Coeurderoy, Deputy Commissioner LaDucer, Jaque Grinberg, and a couple of military SFOR commanders. Harston calmly nodded at me. "We will talk soon," he assured me. I could not help but notice LaDucer's gobsmacked look as I swiftly walked past.

Later, when I tried to play the recorded tape, it was completely garbled, as if there had been a scrambling device in Harston's office.

I never did hear back from Harston. Some months later I would see an email from LaDucer, dated April 24, 2001, in which he reported that Harston did not think I was afforded due process and believed I should have been allowed to continue my mission time but that Harston stated it was DynCorp and the State Department's issue, not his.

Spoken like a career diplomat, I thought; he preferred to sit on the fence.

17

GOING TO THE PRESS
(April 2001)

I spent my last couple of days in Sarajevo talking to as many people as I could, gathering as much information as I could. Some of the most salient insights came from the secretaries, although they were very hesitant to pass along information to me, as they knew it could cost them their jobs. The secretary of the civilian chief of personnel asked Madeleine to tell me that a meeting had taken place among the personnel chief, SRSG Klein, and the U.S. ambassador on the morning I was to be terminated—my pending termination was discussed. The personnel chief had tried to intervene, telling the others that they could not authorize the termination without an investigation. He was told the decision had already been made. If this was DynCorp's problem alone—which was the rationale I had heard from many in the UN—why would the SRSG be discussing me in a meeting with the ambassador?

Another person to feed me information was the policy advisor to the IPTF commissioner, who approached me in the hall of the UN building. Although I had relinquished my official ID, I had received a temporary pass while I turned in the procedural check-out paperwork. I had also dropped off copies of my letter of appeal, along with a request to meet with the commissioner. The policy advisor quietly informed me that the commissioner never received my letter or meeting request, believing that Deputy Commissioner LaDucer had pulled both.

"Did you witness this?" I asked.

"No, but one of the secretaries in the office did."

I decided to pay a visit to LaDucer and asked a Dutch colleague, Theo, to accompany me. Again I concealed my tape recorder in my jacket pocket.

The door to LaDucer's office was halfway open, and I knocked quietly. "Hi...you got a minute?"

I was not who LaDucer expected to see. "How are you doing?" he stumbled. "Yeah, come in."

I introduced Theo, and then LaDucer nervously started rambling about having been off from work and out of town.

"Things kind of went all to hell," I said. "I was hoping to say good-bye and to see if you knew what was going on because I am pretty damn confused actually."

"Well, I have no knowledge of what is going on."

"So you have no knowledge about the letter I sent to the commissioner?"

"No," LaDucer said firmly. "I was out of town."

"Because I tried to get in touch with the commissioner and was informed that perhaps you intercepted my letter—"

"No, I was out of town."

His excuse was getting old. "When did you get back?" I asked.

He paused, then shuffled around some things on his desk to find his day planner. "If I were younger I could tell you the date," he said with a chuckle. He guessed at a few dates before settling on the day, a week earlier.

"Well, if you don't mind, I'd like to give you my version of what happened," I said.

"No," he said. "This is between you and DynCorp, and you and the UN.... This happened in my absence, when I was not here."

"You are the deputy commissioner of this mission, and you don't know what is going on?"

"Listen, I was not here when this started."

I wanted to shout at him, But you're here now! You have one of the top positions in this mission, you are a fellow American DynCorp contractor, and this is going on now, under your command!

"You are going around talking to all these people," LaDucer said, "and I am a little uncomfortable coming back here and finding out—"

"What were you told happened?" I asked, interested to get his version of the story.

"That is really none of your business."

At this point, Theo interrupted. "It's time for us to leave," he said firmly, recognizing that LaDucer was about to lose his temper and that I was on the verge of reaching across the desk and throttling him. Theo was not about to stick around and find out which came first.

———

Later, I paid another visit to John Knight in Logistics to check on the status of my return flight home. DynCorp was now refusing to pay for it, even though, contractually, it was required to do so for monitors who had fulfilled at least a yearlong contract.

"I shouldn't tell you this," John said, "but I had a big upset with someone yesterday and it was about time sheets and I said, 'You know, I had to sack this poor girl just for doing not even a percentage of what you have just done.'"

"And did he get sacked?" I asked.

"No. I don't want to accept this shit and...they don't like me because I tell them that. I am just an old soldier...brought up with a certain way of doing business. The trouble is with me, my brain tells me one thing and my heart tells me another."

"I tell you what, you are a good man," I said.

John then mentioned that the American medal parade was scheduled for tomorrow. I laughed. "I should show up," I said.

"No, stay away!"

"I deserve my medal, I put my time in—"

"Yes, you're entitled to it."

We both laughed at the thought of me showing up demanding that I be presented with a medal. Then I said good-bye to John, knowing I was not likely to see him again.

———

Madeleine Rees was determined to make sure that my remaining time in Bosnia was put to good use. She arranged for me to meet surreptitiously with Angela King, a Jamaican diplomat whose three-decade UN career had taken her around the world on her mission for women's rights—from South Africa, where she was praised by Nelson Mandela, to her current appointment by Secretary-General Kofi Annan as Special Advisor on Gender Issues and Advancement of Women.

In the evening, in an unoccupied office in the UN building, Madeleine and I met with King. I had a lump in my throat during our entire meeting, knowing that Madeleine was putting her own job on the line by setting this up. By this point I was getting fed up with the whole thing—I was trying to keep my temper in check and hold back tears at the same time. I detailed the cases implicating IPTF and the lack of follow-up. King listened intently, forehead creased, not saying a thing. I had prepared copies of a few pertinent reports and files and gave them to her. She paged through them, then looked me hard in the eye.

"Why have you not gone to the press with this?" she asked.

I was taken aback by her response.

She continued. "You need to keep talking, and keep talking as widely as you can. Be safe, but do not give up. Good luck, and we are behind you and support you." Although I had hoped she would help me spearhead these efforts, I knew I should heed her advice, even if it was all on my own.

Afterward, Madeleine and I snuck out of the building—no one knew she had arranged this meeting, and she wanted to keep it that way. That night the thought that kept circling in my mind was to call the American ambassador. If he had indeed been informed that my termination was to occur, then I wanted to get his firsthand account of why no one had intervened and if there was anything that could still be done—especially since he knew of my work with human trafficking, a cause that his wife cared about passionately. I tossed and turned in bed, which was actually the couch of my Swedish colleague and friend Lotta Gustafsson. I had been camping out at her place for the past few days, since I no longer felt safe staying alone at my accommodations.

I barely slept, and the next day, I mustered up the nerve to call the ambassador. After being patched through to his mobile as he was on a tarmac, it was too loud to have any meaningful conversation. He suggested we schedule a meeting for the following week, and that was that. It was time for me to recognize that I had done all I could do for now and that, for my own safety, I needed to leave Bosnia. The rest of the day was a whirlwind: Thor showed up, talking of wire-taps and possible retaliation. I stayed at his accommodations that night and drove out of Sarajevo first thing the next morning. Jan had flown into Zagreb, and I met him at the airport. When I saw him, I nearly collapsed in his arms, finally allowing myself to cry. I slept almost the entire way as he drove us back to Holland.

———

Madeleine had also heeded King's words and had been active—although discreet—in talking to the press. The article that broke the story of my termination came out a few months later via the Institute for War and Peace Reporting and, locally, in Sarajevo's largest newspaper, *Oslobođenje*.[1] The headline was: "The UN Mission in Bosnia Comes under Fire for Allegedly Trying to Cover up a Prostitution Scandal."

A former spokesperson for the Organization for Security and Cooperation in Europe and a graduate student in human rights at Columbia University, Tanya Domi reported the story. Although she misspelled my last name, everything else was dead-on target. The article began: "The United Nations mission in Bosnia-Herzegovina may face an investigation following charges that it sought to cover up media reports implicating its officials in selling women into prostitution. UN headquarters in Sarajevo has denied the claims but acknowledged that several members of its staff have been sacked for misconduct. The charges were first aired by Kathy Balkovac [*sic*], an American police officer and a former UN human rights investigator....Balkovac alleged that extensive trafficking of women into prostitution had been carried out by UN personnel, NATO troops and other international officials in Bosnia, along with the local police."

The article went on to detail how I was determined to have been stressed and burned out, and then terminated by DynCorp. Domi reported how the office of the High Commissioner for Human Rights in Sarajevo demanded that there be an investigation that would be carried out "in an open and transparent manner and that the reports should be made public..." and that punishment for anyone found guilty should be "commensurate with the gravity of the offences."

Noting that prostitution is illegal in Bosnia, the article continued: "Doug Coffman, spokesperson for the UN in Sarajevo, said a few weeks ago that he was not aware of any UN investigation into Balkovac's charges. He said that only one UN officer was found guilty of paying for a prostitute. In a press statement in May, Klein denied all allegations that the UN mission had concealed reports of misconduct. 'During my tenure, there have been no cover-ups and I have implemented a zero-tolerance policy regarding sexual and other serious misconduct,' he said in the statement. 'Following due process, the UN has investigated all allegations of misconduct in a fair, thorough and timely manner.' "

Domi also interviewed Martina Vandenberg of Human Rights Watch. Vandenberg said: "Trafficking in women is called the 'dirty secret of UN interventions around the world—the nasty underbelly that no one wants to confront. . . . None of these allegations come as a surprise."

Domi reiterated that prostitution is illegal in Bosnia, and that an estimated "200,000 to 300,000 women are sold into prostitution from former communist bloc countries in Eastern Europe and the former Soviet Union to Western Europe and North America annually."

This article on my struggle with DynCorp and the situation in Bosnia would be the first of many.

18

THE KHAKI DUFFEL BAG
(April 2001–April 2002)

Jan and I drove from Zagreb to his apartment in s'Graveland, which means "land of the dukes," in the Netherlands. Soon after I settled in, I took Madeleine Rees's advice and called Karen Bailey, the solicitor in the United Kingdom whom she had recommended. Karen was the first African Caribbean woman solicitor to set up her own legal practice in Birmingham, England. A few weeks later, when I made the trip to her office, it looked as if she had just moved in, with teetering stacks of cardboard boxes and papers strewn everywhere. I asked if this was a new space.

"No," she said offhandedly, "it's always like this." Karen was in her mid-forties and had a quick, broad smile and chatty, informal demeanor. At her desk, she pushed papers into piles to carve out a little space. "Shall we have a look?"

I opened the khaki Eddie Bauer duffel bag that had traveled with me from Nebraska to Bosnia to England and pulled from it a thick three-ring binder that landed with a thud on Karen's desk. Her eyes grew wide and she looked at the binder then back at me, speechless.

Document, document, document! I had spent countless hours—with the help of Jan, who, in the Dutch Intelligence, was no stranger to evidence gathering—organizing the binder with dozens of tabs: Names, Dates, Cases, Letters, Contracts, People, and Positions. Arguably, we had covered every conceivable who, what, when, and where of this case—only the why was missing. Neither I, nor Jan, nor my colleagues from the UN, nor the handful of friends I had made at DynCorp could come up with a plausible motive for this widespread cover-up of mission personnel involvement in human trafficking.

As Karen began flipping through the pages, I described the previous two years: the disappearing files, the thwarted investigations, the threats, my eventual demotion, and then firing. She scribbled down notes. After a couple of hours, she finally pushed away from her desk and leaned back in her chair.

"You have a very strong case," she said. "You made what I believe can be determined to be a protected disclosure. In other words, you blew the whistle, and they created some reason to have you fired. But you need to know, no matter how good your case may be, you will not win a million dollars. We have caps in place, and those types of awards are simply inconceivable in the UK." She paused, then looked pointedly at me. "But I can assure you this will be handled promptly. You will be heard."

That was what I wanted most. I wanted DynCorp's contractors' involvement in human trafficking exposed, I wanted the U.S. State Department to know how it was being represented abroad, and I wanted the American taxpayers to see how our dollars were being spent.

At the end of June 2001, Karen filed a lawsuit on my behalf against DynCorp for unfair dismissal due to a protected disclosure (whistle blowing). My hearing date was set for almost a year later, in April 2002. The case would go before the Employment Tribunal, the executive agency in the United Kingdom's Department of Trade and Industry, which hears over 100,000 cases annually. Three independent professionals formed each deciding body. As is common practice, Karen enlisted a barrister specializing in employment and discrimination to represent me before the Tribunal. Karen and the barrister would handle my case on a contingency basis: If we won, they would receive a third of what was awarded. They would get nothing if we lost.

During the summer of 2001, with Jan at my side, I dragged the khaki duffel bag to London, to a red brick, white-columned building nestled on an ivy-covered courtyard, to meet barrister Stephanie Harrison of Garden Court Chambers.

Stephanie was in her thirties, and two things were immediately apparent: She was quite smart and quite disheveled. Her sandy hair was in a half-loose bun haphazardly stabbed with a hair clip that kept falling down. Her skirt was remarkably wrinkled, and her shoes were very sensibly flat. She walked as if she were in a hurry, even though we were just moving down the hall to her office. Yet, there was something forceful and commanding about her; she was very direct and very real. It took hours for me to give my statement of account; as it grew dark, I could see the streetlamps illuminating the Thames River from Stephanie's office window. Our stomachs growling, we took a break for a quick bite to eat, but when we returned to the building, the wrought-iron gates surrounding it were locked. Stephanie seemed oblivious to the fact that the gates were locked around this time every evening. "Hmm," she said matter-of-factly, "my key is inside."

Jan and I nervously looked at each other—my duffel bag was inside the building, and I was not about to leave without it. Without hesitation, Jan—his friends called him MacGyver for good reason—scaled the gates and quickly determined how to force the lock and let us in. "Well, that was handy," Stephanie commented as we headed inside.

Back upstairs, she finished photocopying my files and then snapped shut my binder. "Your case illustrates a serious miscarriage of justice," she said. "I'm quite impressed with your investigative measures. Commendable doggedness."

I thanked her and packed up my bag. Although we would continue working together over the phone, I would not see Stephanie again until the trial. As Jan and I stood to go, she said, "You will have to encounter them all at the tribunal, you know."

I nodded; yes, I knew.

"But," she continued, "Karen and I will carry the load now. You're not to worry."

Despite her bouts of flightiness, I left feeling relieved, as if my backup had finally arrived.

————

If trying a case in the United States is akin to an oral exam, a UK tribunal case is a take-home essay. Our document contained an explanatory booklet—several pages outlining, step by step, the sequence of events and my grievances. Less than a week after filing suit, we received DynCorp's attorneys' response, in which they— the "Respondent"—addressed each point in my—the "Applicant's"— explanation. Their answers were littered with the phrase: "The Respondent does not have any direct operational authority for US Police Monitors in UN missions." This was my point exactly: No one, not DynCorp, not the UN, not the State Department, wanted to claim responsibility for the actions of the IPTF.

News of my suit promptly made its way to Bosnia. In July 2001 the mission responded with a special press conference, introducing the UN's new Special Trafficking Operations Program (STOP). SRSG Klein named a French journalist, Celhia de Lavarene, to be the advisor on gender policy and head of the STOP team. She would lead international and local police on brothel raids throughout the country—despite the fact that, by her own admission, she had no policing background and no prior experience in working directly with victims of human trafficking.[1]

STOP estimated that approximately 25 percent of the women and girls working in nightclubs and bars were trafficked; however, Martina Vandenberg, in 2002's Human Rights Watch Report on Bosnia, later countered STOP's projection: "NGO [nongovernmental organization] experts working to stop trafficking in Bosnia and Herzegovina, cautioning that the statistics remain woefully unreliable, estimated that as many as 2,000 women and girls from the former Soviet Union and Eastern Europe have found themselves trapped in Bosnian brothels."[2] This was far more than 25 percent.

Over the next two years, STOP raided between 240 to 470 premises (the numbers vary according to UN-released statistics and statistics presented in de Lavarene's biography on the STOP website). Veteran BBC journalist Sue Lloyd-Roberts and a camera crew followed de Lavarene and the STOP team on a day of raids in Bosnia. Their documentary, Boys Will Be Boys,[3] aired in Europe a year after STOP had been in action. In one brothel, the team found ten young women, no brothel owner in sight.

"The girls did not look very pleased to see you," Lloyd-Roberts said.

"They're afraid," De Lavarene replied. "Most of them don't have a passport. One said she lost it two days ago, which I don't believe. What I believe is that she never had one."

Lloyd-Roberts asked why so few sought help.

"Because they're afraid, because it takes time, because the bar owners are telling them that we are going to sell them, buy them, put them in jail, that we are using them. That's the problem," De Lavarene said.

Lloyd-Roberts then surmised that the problem could also be that the girls were confused. She narrated: "Some policemen come to the bars at night, others come as their rescuers by day." Roberts went on to describe how she and the BBC camera crew, this time without the STOP team, went back to the raided bar a few days later, only to find that it was business as usual.

In an interview with Madeleine Rees, Lloyd-Roberts asked if the raids achieved anything. Madeleine shook her head and stated that brothel raids alone did not work, simply because traffickers were not that stupid. They would continue to force women into prostitution, only they would become sneakier about it, moving farther underground. So instead of an advertised nightclub, they would have an innocuous room above a restaurant or a woman would be delivered to an apartment or a motel.

So why then, Lloyd-Roberts pushed, do the raids take place?

"Show and tell," Madeleine answered. "So that we look as if we've dealt with the problem, because if it's underground, then it's not an identifiable problem, so we can move on. [The] United Nations says, yet again, it has done something, when in fact it has not done something."

At the conclusion of the UN mission in Bosnia in December 2002, STOP would claim that it had closed 142 brothels, interviewed 1,600 women and girls, rescued 265 victims, and repatriated 186 victims to their home countries.[4] Why, I wondered, did only a fraction of the rescued victims actually make it home? Given STOP's initial (and perhaps quite low) projection that 25 percent of women in brothels had likely been trafficked, why were only 8 percent of the women found during raids repatriated?

My human rights colleagues who were still on the mission, including some IPTF members on the STOP team, remained in touch with me, expressing their consistent frustration and also keeping me up to date on news from the ground. I received a flurry of emails from these colleagues in October 2001, after Klein was interviewed by Tim Sebastian for BBC Hardtalk, a news show that covered breaking or controversial news items. Sebastian cornered Klein on his conflicting evidence. "You've had UN officials engaged in trafficking women," he said.

"Not true at all," Klein responded.

"These are clear allegations," Sebastian pushed.

Klein stated, "Allegations and rumors and hearsay...I can categorically state that not a single United Nations Police Officer since the beginning of the Mission, and 10,000 of them have been there, has been involved in the trafficking of a single woman."

"There are people who have gone against that," Sebastian said. "Richard Monk, for instance, who ran the UN police operation in Bosnia until 1999, he said there were dreadful things going on by UN Police Officers from a number of countries...officers were having sex with minors and prostitutes. That cuts directly across what you've just told me."

But Klein held firm. "Maybe during his tenure, not during mine. No international police officer has been involved in the trafficking of women," he insisted.

"What about the allegations of Kathryn Bolkovac, former UN police officer?" Sebastian asked.

Klein responded, "Every allegation is investigated, every single one of them had been, and when the investigators came they went through each case file. Because we had rumors going back to 1991 about people trafficking."[5]

I nearly hit the roof when I read the transcript of this interview. Just whose case files was Klein referring to? I oversaw the Gender Desk, and my case files, as well as those from my human rights colleagues, contained far more than rumors; they were full of documented and corroborated witness statements, photographs, and even surveillance tapes, such as the report that David Lamb had fumed about, wherein a Tuzla narcotics officer had risked his life going undercover. My files had been conveniently lost in the Internal

Affairs department, not investigated. Likewise, the investigators that Klein was referring to had been sent at the request of the UN High Commissioner for Human Rights. Their mandate was to conduct a preliminary inquiry into the involvement of IPTF in human trafficking in regard to the case that David Lamb and then Rosario Ioanna had been trying to work. These two investigators, from the Office of Internal Oversight, never contacted Lamb, who had since completed his mission, nor were they able to interview any victims since they had all been transported out of Bosnia months earlier. After a week the investigators concluded there were "insufficient grounds to move ahead with a full-blown criminal investigation."[5]

Sebastian continued to hammer Klein, questioning how the SRSG's assessment could vary so drastically from the highly respected former IPTF commissioner, Richard Monk. Klein kept to his line that Monk may have had problems, but there were no longer any issues.

"But it just doesn't go away overnight," Sebastian said.

"No, but 24 of them have been sent home since I've been there," Klein said. "I will not tolerate it and they have been sent home, including 6 Americans."

His mention of six Americans seemed to come out of nowhere, and I wondered what he was referring to. I received a prompt answer from my former colleague Marja, a Dutch human rights IPTF investigator, who emailed me on October 31, 2001, that six high-level IPTF who worked at Main HQ recently had been implicated by several trafficked women during another investigation. Before any real investigation could take place, the women were repatriated to their hometowns in Romania. A few dedicated Internal Affairs officers requested permission from Klein to travel there to interview the victims properly, but Klein refused them clearance. Instead, in an atypical move for the head of the mission, Klein himself went to Romania to conduct an interview with one of the trafficking victims. This was all Marja knew.

Once again Sue Lloyd-Roberts was on the beat, and she detailed the circumstances in *Boys Will Be Boys*. Lloyd-Roberts had all the access I wished I had had and asked all the questions that had been hammering away at me. She located one of the trafficking victims, Alina, whom Klein had interviewed in Romania. According to Alina, an Argentinean IPTF officer, who had been an infrequent client of hers, paid 2,000 Deutsch Marks (more than $1,300) to get her out of the brothel. "But what's intriguing about her story," Lloyd-Roberts narrated, "is that when the head of the UN Mission, Jacques Paul Klein, came to Romania on official business, he sent for Alina to meet him in Bucharest, where he showed her an album with the photographs of twenty IPTF policemen." Lloyd-Roberts asked Alina how many of the IPTF officers she was able to identify.

Alina responded that out of the twenty pictures she was shown, she could identify all but three IPTF officers. "There were many who used to come to the bar," Alina said, "the IPTF had known for years about the girls and the problems but did nothing at all."

Back in Sarajevo, Lloyd-Roberts visited UN HQ, following up directly with Klein. He acknowledged on camera that he was aware of the problem of internationals using brothels and insisted, "They were sent home." But in fact, Lloyd-Roberts countered, Alina had identified numerous IPTF monitors who paid for services with her, but only one person—the Argentine who had bought her freedom—had been sent home. Klein disagreed, first indicating that he thought Alina had identified only one person. His conviction—as well as his justification for his actions—would grow significantly stronger as the conversation went on.

"[T]hese are not judicial interviews in the sense of a Western court," Klein said. "We have no executive authority. I can't swear you. She identified one person, I believe that individual was disciplined and sent home."

"We spoke to her two days ago and she said she identified seventeen," Lloyd-Roberts replied.

"That's a direct and outright lie," Klein insisted.

"Well, it's only her word against yours," said Lloyd-Roberts.

Klein insisted he had "the document," but when Lloyd-Roberts asked to see it, UN officials would not give it to her. She asked Klein: "Are you protecting them?"

"Well, that's rather rude," Klein scoffed. "I mean I thought you were a serious journalist. She did not identify seventeen people to me. She identified one Argentine and one possible other one but she wasn't sure; that was all. So let's not get carried away. These people, based on how you ask the question, how you stimulate the conversation, will say anything you want."

It was infuriating to hear how Klein belittled trafficking victims, referring to them as "these people." His rationale also did not support his own cause—if "people" like Alina were categorically unreliable witnesses, why would Klein spend his time personally interviewing her, especially without the assistance of a specialist in trafficking victims and without bothering to see if the other nineteen women associated with this case could provide corroborating evidence?

Lloyd-Roberts was not buying his story either, and she went back to Madeleine, asking why the head of the mission would personally interview a girl who'd been trafficked.

"I cannot imagine. I really cannot imagine why," Madeleine said. "[I]t's outside the jurisdiction, it certainly would not fall within the standard operating procedures. I think if you ask Klein that he would say it was because he wanted to find out for himself the truth of the extent of the involvement of IPTF in trafficking. It's very difficult to understand the rationale behind it...if you have that seniority and that position, you don't go and interview someone who's been trafficked because someone who's been trafficked does need support, does need counseling, is not exactly in the sound shape to give evidence in that sort of manner."

"So it was an extraordinary thing to do?" Lloyd-Roberts asked.

"It was extraordinary and entirely inappropriate," Madeleine said, "entirely inappropriate."[6]

———

At the end of September 2001 I received an email from the office of Representative Doug Bereuter, First District of Nebraska. He was interested in my "recent stay in Bosnia and [my] future plans" and was requesting an appointment to meet. Since I was planning to be in Lincoln over Christmas, we scheduled a day that I would come to his office.

When Bereuter and I met, I began by explaining what I had gone through and what DynCorp was doing. He did not seem shocked. I asked if there was a way he could help. He paused a moment, then said that about the only thing he might be able to do was to get the General Accounting Office to look into any potential waste and fraud. While this was not along the direct lines I was hoping for, I thought this still could be a valuable angle, as I also had heard about allegations of gouging. I thanked him, but after the exchange of a few friendly follow-up emails, I never heard back from Representative Bereuter.

My legal team and I continued working diligently to build my case. The British tribunal system, as Karen had described it, was far more prompt than the U.S. judicial system, and my tribunal date was set for April 22, 2002.

———

Karen was in touch with Texas attorney Kevin Glasheen, who was handling the case of *Ben Johnston v. DynCorp Inc.* Johnston—the aircraft mechanic who had blown the whistle on his superiors who were buying and selling underage, trafficked women, distributing a "rape video," and trafficking in weapons—also had been abruptly terminated.

Since he first filed his suit in August 2000 (which was just after I'd been appointed to the Gender Desk), Johnston alleged that he had received repeated and serious death threats and was forced to move to a different town. According to the *Dallas Morning News*: "Most newcomers arrive in town as Texas Tech University students or employees. Ben D. Johnston and his wife, Denisa, came to west Texas to escape the Serbian mafia....Returning to west Texas seemed natural after gangsters in Tuzla, Bosnia-Herzegovina, threatened his life for blowing the whistle on their sale of young women and firearms to Americans working on U.S. Army bases."[7]

Because Johnston was contracted through a different division of DynCorp and via the Department of Defense (I was contracted via the State Department), his contract was governed by U.S. law. Glasheen had filed the case in Fort Worth and was alleging that DynCorp engaged in racketeering in violation of the Racketeer Influenced and Corrupt Organizations (RICO) Act. The suit also alleged that DynCorp breached Johnston's three-year contract when he was fired after two-and-a-half years. Glasheen asked if I would be interested in giving a deposition, and we scheduled a date for that summer, after my scheduled tribunal hearing. That date also happened to be my birthday, and there was no better gift I could give myself.

With my tribunal hearing quickly approaching, I secured written witness statements, both regarding my character and the events in Bosnia, from my fellow mission colleagues: Bo, Lotta, Jan, and Madeleine; the chief of police from Lincoln; and the former IPTF commissioner, Richard Monk, who—as BBC journalist Tim

Sebastian had pointed out—had not been afraid to speak out about the issues of human trafficking on international missions.

My attorneys and I felt that Madeleine would be an excellent in-person witness—however, her UN immunity would prevent her from testifying. I brought this up with Madeleine, and she surprised me by volunteering to file to get her UN immunity waived in order to testify. This was a courageous act—in going up against DynCorp, she was essentially going up against the mission, the UN, and SRSG Klein. The UN world was not big enough for this action to go unnoticed. This was very telling of the kind of person Madeleine was: she would risk her job and her career to appear at my trial and to put on record the abuses of power she had witnessed.

As part of the exchange of documents that were to be presented as evidence, DynCorp's discovery materials were delivered to my attorneys. Its documents contained a surprisingly sparse amount of actual evidence. They included personal emails that had been solicited specifically for the trial, after I already had been terminated. It appeared that my superiors, such as DynCorp site manager Pascal Budge, had tried to dig up any dirt that they could on me from my fellow monitors. When none could be found, apparently Budge tried to solicit information, calling around to see if anyone had any disparaging information regarding me or my work. DynCorp produced two emails addressed to Budge. The first, dated July 16, 2001, was from a monitor who had received a promotion that I had also applied for.

The monitor explained to Budge: "I sat down after our brief phone call yesterday and remembered a conversation I had with Kathy...here is a synopsis that may be of some, if any, use to your efforts." The monitor went on to describe that he did not know me but had sat with me one day at the UN cafeteria. When he told me his position, I said that I had also applied for that post. He replied, "Just be glad there is a God the job can be a real pain in the ass!!"

He then reported that I said that I did not really want the job, I just wanted out of Sarajevo. My statement caused him a "feeling of self worth diminished a bit." He concluded his email with: "Other than that, we did not speak about work again. I don't know if this is of any significance but I thought you would like to know." He then went on to be far more negative about DynCorp than about me. "Truthfully, I don't always agree with UN policy here," he wrote. "I get so frustrated sometimes I could go postal....I will always stand up for anyone who feels they have been done wrong or is just trying to right a wrong, but there are ways to do it without crippling a damn good effort by their Country men and women. Good Luck."

The next email to Budge was from Dennis LaDucer, on May 3, 2001, in which he offered a list of "how [he] would describe the employee." This list contained negative attributes with absolutely no references, specifics, or circumstances for backup. LaDucer asserted that I was "politically naive," which he said was evidenced by my inability to comprehend the impact of my "Guilty Conscience" email on the U.S. Embassy, the mission, and the State Department.

Also within the bundle of files from DynCorp was a curious email from the Legal Department advising that I be reinstated and that proper disciplinary procedure be conducted—indicating that Budge and Popwell had not adhered to the recommended steps. If they wanted to score for our team, we were happy to let them.

A week before the trial, DynCorp's attorney, Peter Holt, called Karen Bailey and offered a settlement of approximately $30,000. My first instinct was to burst out laughing. Karen reminded me that the offer was far from measly: The average award in a tribunal is a third of that. Still, I instructed Karen to turn it down.

"Just so we're clear," she told me, "I'm not advising that you should take the settlement, but I do need to reiterate that there is no guarantee you will win this case and, regardless of the outcome, it will not be pleasant to endure."

"I don't want the settlement," I replied. Not that I did not need the money. Since my dismissal, I had been working as a data-entry clerk near Schiphol Airport in the Netherlands. It was the only job I could find since my name and law enforcement record had been blighted. Thirty thousand dollars would have been a boon to my finances—my meager savings had long ago been exhausted by child support, then three college tuitions and two graduate programs. Still, I simply was not interested in settling with DynCorp. I told Karen that even if DynCorp counteroffered, to turn it down. "No matter what they offer," I emphasized, "even if they add another zero to the figure, tell them I'm not interested. And I'd like you to add a 'go to hell.' "

Karen chuckled. "I will get the message to them."

On April 21, 2002, the day before my tribunal hearing, I leaned against the rails of the ferry as we chugged across the English Channel. The diesel vapors stung my nose as I took a deep breath, trying to calm my nerves—but it was no use; my hands would not stop shaking. Jan stood next to me, knowing there was nothing he could say that would help. We gave each other the same pained look we had been exchanging since we had left our cozy attic apartment in a small village outside Amsterdam that morning.

I thought back to my time with the Lincoln Police Force, back to one of my arrests, which had been written up in the *Lincoln Journal Star* in 1998. Stephanie and Karen had included the article in documents submitted to the tribunal as evidence of my police experience prior to going to Bosnia.

The arrest was of a twenty-year-old man, Douglass, for a traffic violation.

When Bolkovac was walking [Douglass] to her cruiser, he pushed her and ran away. She chased him, and a struggle ensued. During the struggle, Douglass put Bolkovac in a headlock, and Bolkovac bit Douglass to get him to release her. Douglass released Bolkovac and started to run. She tackled him, and he started kicking her head and shoulders. Bolkovac finally got him into custody, but not before he broke her collarbone and injured her neck and throat. Officers later found a fannypack in the front seat of Douglass' car that had a bag of methamphetamine and a 9mm pistol.

The image of a strong officer fighting back was in stark contrast to how I felt about myself now. Yes, I was still fighting back, but, as Jan had written in his witness statement, which had been submitted to the tribunal during the review process, I was a different person:

[T]his has all had an enormous effect on Ms. Bolkovac's well being and feeling of safety and security.... [S]he was nothing like that confident, self-assured woman I knew before. This showed itself during the next couple of weeks in sleeplessness, loss of appetite, edgy emotions and distant moods, which I had never experienced in her before. Eventually she even lost the appetite for athletics and working out, activities that she had regularly undertaken and enjoyed before.

Jan was my main support throughout this ordeal. I tried not to get my children too involved in the details as they would have worried and not understood the full scope of the situation. They knew the basics of what was happening to me and knew I was dealing with a very serious situation. Jan's coolheaded and soothing manner had a calming effect on me as the events unfolded.

When we reached the dock, I waited as Jan drove his car, a compact Opel, up from the bowels of the ferry. I got in and stared blankly out the window. Jan reached for my hand as we continued our silent journey to the tribunal in Southampton, where *Bolkovac v. DynCorp* was to be heard.

19

TRIBUNAL
(April 22–23, 2002)

I had never been to Southampton, England, before, and all I knew about it was the unsettling fact that it was the departure point of the Titanic. "It didn't sink here," Jan quietly emphasized as we passed an imposing memorial to the perished crew.

The tribunal was held at Dukes Keep, which I expected would be a stately building, like a traditional courthouse. Instead, it was a drab, gated structure that reminded me of a low-security prison.

In the lot, Jan turned off the car, and we sat quietly for a moment. I did not want to see them, the DynCorp men, my former employers: the VP of European Operations, the deputy commissioner, the contingent commander, the Bosnia site manager. They had tried everything they could to ruin me. Jan took my face in his hands and gave me a long stare. "It's your turn now," he said, then nodded and popped the trunk.

Out came the khaki duffel bag, and I held onto it tightly as we headed toward the building. As we got closer, we saw a handful of reporters and photographers milling around by the entrance.

"Are you Kathy Bolkovac?" someone called out. I nodded, and the flashes went off. One reporter handed me his business card.

"I'm from *The Times* of London," he said. "I've been following your case, and I'd be very interested to talk with you further."

In the lobby, Karen was waiting for us, trailing a case of her own that contained copies of my documents. She strode over to us and whisked us past the press, who followed us into the courthouse. The reporters were allowed to attend the hearing but were barred from taking photographs in the building or the courtroom.

"Do you have the tapes?" Karen asked.

"Of course," I said.

Karen led us to the third floor, to what looked like nothing more than a conference room with the tables arranged in a horseshoe so that the plaintiffs' table faced the defendants' table head on. The room was empty but for us, and I set about laying out my materials while Jan went to sit in the row of chairs behind the tables. From my bag I took the binder and placed it in front of my chair. Jan had transferred all the tapes I had secretly recorded onto a single CD, and I set that alongside the binder. Last, I pulled out some stapled pages that I had printed from the Internet.

It was amazing what news articles and court cases a simple Internet search had turned up. Sure, all the monitors had come with some kind of history, and every DynCorp employee—myself included—had his or her own reasons for choosing mission life, but what I had uncovered about some of the men who were about to face me was damning. They were the kinds of things that should have immediately ruled out any candidate for employment, had DynCorp done even the most basic of background checks. I placed those stapled pages front and center.

Just under the hour, Barrister Stephanie Harrison hurried in and slid onto the chair next to me. She brushed some strands of hair from her face and looked at me with a warm smile. "Be yourself. Tell your story," she said, and gave my arm a squeeze. I was suddenly very grateful she was there, and then I looked down to see massive runs in both legs of her stockings. *Well*, I thought, *it could be worse.* I could also have runs in my stockings.

Just then I heard deep voices nearby, and the door opened. A wave of energy washed over me. Jan was right. It was my turn now.

———

American Contingent Commander Jamie Popwell, DynCorp Site Manager Pascal Budge, and DynCorp Junior Vice President of European Operations Spence Wickham, all in business suits and bright ties, paraded into the room. I had been lethargic and depressed for nearly a year as I waited for this day—but seeing them, with their smug expressions, started my adrenaline flowing again. No cameras were allowed in the room, but a few reporters were seated in the back, quietly taking notes. I was glad they were there; the press had been my biggest ally so far.

John Knight, DynCorp Logistics Manager, had been on the original witness list for DynCorp, but he was not present, and I saw his name had been removed from the revised list. I wondered what had happened to him. Watching the other side, with its three witnesses, I wished I had someone on my side to put on the stand. We had collected excellent written statements, which were entered in as evidence, but because of a lack of funds and because my sources were all over Europe, it was not feasible to have an in-person witness line-up. However, there was still Madeleine. So far she had not received any notice of waiver of her immunity from the UN; we were hoping she still would be able to show up at the tribunal.

While DynCorp's attorney had previously received transcripts of my tape-recorded conversations, that morning, in a private room, would be the first time the attorneys and DynCorp crew would hear the actual recording of my encounter with Popwell at the Main HQ elevator. The tape had also been made available to the tribunal, and I assumed the members had listened to it in their chambers. Although

Popwell had even used recollected portions of the "conversation" in his previously submitted witness statement, reading the words was no substitute for actually hearing the fierceness of his voice, his tone indicating that he was one step away from physically striking me.

The DynCorp legal team consisted of a barrister and solicitor, both of whom looked extremely young. Prior to the start of the trial, the DynCorp barrister, Ben Elkington, asked to meet with Stephanie. Jan and I were ushered into a separate room to wait while the barristers talked. After more than a half hour, Stephanie at last appeared. She informed us that Elkington had conceded that, indeed, the dismissal was procedurally unfair in that I was not given adequate notice of the allegations against me, nor adequate opportunity to answer the allegations, nor an opportunity to appeal. However, DynCorp still maintained that I was dismissed for gross misconduct and that the outcome would have been the same even if there had been no procedural unfairness. Elkington also conceded that my "Guilty Conscience" email—which would be referred to throughout the tribunal as the "email of October 9"—may or may not be considered a "protected disclosure" and that it was my burden to prove that my dismissal was for whistleblowing and not for falsifying time sheets.

I looked at this as my first small victory. We returned to the main room to begin the tribunal. Stephanie stated our position: unfair dismissal because of a protected disclosure under the terms of the Public Interest Disclosure Act of 1998.

The tribunal panel consisted of three members: Chairman C. E. H. Twiss, Mrs. D. Hackforth, and Mr. M. Heckford. I watched them closely, trying to get a read on who they were and what they were thinking. I did not know anything about them or how they had been chosen to be on the panel, nor would I ever have the chance to talk with them. Mrs. Hackforth looked very refined and polished, with a sharp business suit and short, silver hair that was perfectly in place; she struck me as very smart and to the point. Mr. Heckford seemed more salt of the earth; I imagined that perhaps he was a union foreman. He had a kind demeanor and seemed to express empathy at times throughout my testimony, even though it was clear that he was trying to remain neutral.

Mr. Twiss called the hearing to order and read out the basis of the claim, noting the new admission by DynCorp regarding the unfair dismissal, which Stephanie was able to later read and discuss in the court. This was important news, so one reporter scurried out, apparently wanting to make an early edition, writing as he walked out of the room. Twiss went on to explain the details of how the witnesses would be asked to testify under oath by swearing on the Bible or making a written and verbal pledge to the tribunal.

I chose the Bible. Then I began by reading my prepared statement, hoping my voice was not quivering. If it was, it was from anger, not fear, and certainly not tears. I was determined to remain confident and strong. My statement included a description of events and ended with these words:

> It should be noted that all of the men involved in my demotion and termination had made a career out of mission life and most are still working for DynCorp. I have been unable to return to international law enforcement in any capacity, even though many organizations are using my case and experiences as an example and model...on how to improve mission policing and human rights investigations.[1]

First to be sworn in on the DynCorp side was Spence Wickham. He stated that the grounds for my dismissal were consistent with the handling of three other monitors who were dismissed by DynCorp for gross misconduct, specifically time-sheet fraud. We were prepared with a rebuttal: Not only had we investigated the three other cases of time-sheet fraud, but I had worked with one of the monitors, who had been a station commander and had gone absent without leave for approximately twenty-three days. When he finally returned, he attempted to lie about his absence. The UN, following proper procedure, conducted an investigation through Internal Affairs and assigned an officer to assist the commander in his defense. The commander was reassigned to the Zenica Station—where I was—while his disciplinary hearing was pending, and he received full pay in the interim. When he at last admitted to having been absent, he was terminated, although his name was never slandered with accusations of fraud. One day he was simply gone, and no one whispered about it or emailed rumors back and forth.

Stephanie asked Wickham about DynCorp's standard disciplinary procedure, and his account of the steps was accurate. She noted that the system was fair and comprehensive yet, in my case, it was not followed. Wickham admitted that if the procedure had been followed, the outcome might have been different.[2]

Next up was Site Manager Pascal Budge. Like Wickham, he was a career DynCorp employee, not a contracted monitor. He had a vested interest in DynCorp's overall success in Bosnia.

"Was the Applicant's redeployment a demotion?" Stephanie asked.

"I can't deny that it was a demotion," Budge responded.[3]

Budge then denied having any knowledge of my email of October 9. However, I had a copy (which Stephanie entered into evidence) of an email from him, sent a week after my email, where he had forwarded my email on to two colleagues with the subject "Kathryn Bolkovac," and the message: "This email was entitled, 'Do not read this if you have a weak stomach or guilty conscience.'"

Budge then testified that he had been made aware that the UN Personnel Office was carrying out a "preliminary review" of my time sheets—eleven months after the leave date in question. Apparently, this was not something Budge felt DynCorp needed to take a role in (rightly so, according to standard operating procedure), nor was it seemingly that urgent, for he soon left on a monthlong vacation. As Stephanie summed it up for the panel, the following week, while he was out of the country and over rushed international telephone conversations, Budge instructed a logistics manager to terminate me without due process. The termination letter had already been typed up when I arrived for the meeting that Budge and DynCorp referred to as my "opportunity to present evidence to the contrary."

Stephanie asked Budge, "Was there some reason that the monitor's behavior was so blatant that the action could not have waited for proper procedures to be followed upon your return? Why was there such a rush to get the Applicant out of the country and out of her job?"

Budge did not have an answer. He shook his head as he struggled for words, eventually arriving at his fallback phrase: "I don't recall." The tribunal panel members' pens were flying as they took notes. Stephanie questioned Budge's relationship to J. Michael Stiers, and Budge noted that prior to going to work for DynCorp, he had been a police officer in Aurora, Colorado, where Stiers was his fellow officer. Stephanie reinforced the point that Budge was involved in recruitment and that Stiers had been named the highest-ranking American official on the mission. I glanced at the stapled pages in front of me: The link between the two men would become far more pertinent when Former Deputy Commissioner Stiers testified. I had been a bit surprised that Stiers was not present in the DynCorp line-up, although he was still on the witness list. Stephanie informed me that it was our right to call him to testify at any point. Also conspicuously missing from the witnesses was Dennis LaDucer.

Chairman Twiss called a lunch break, and the parties gathered at opposite ends of the hall. I asked Stephanie and Karen if they knew what had happened to John Knight, but all they could say was that he was no longer involved in the tribunal. John clearly had been DynCorp's fall guy—there had to be more to the story of why he was no longer going to testify. Jan and I quickly looked up John's phone number in Britain. Despite the fact that I had recorded my conversations with him and submitted them as evidence, the old soldier seemed happy to hear from me and said he had been following the newspaper reports on the lawsuit.

"I no longer work for DynCorp," he told me. I cringed. He had been encouraged to resign, it seemed, and as for testifying, he told DynCorp he refused to do so. He said he was sorry he had not assisted me more while everything was happening in Bosnia, and he wished me all the best.

When the hearing resumed, it was my turn to take the stand. Unlike in the United States, there was no witness box, so I remained seated at the table. Elkington insinuated that I had not seriously looked for employment in the time that had elapsed and claimed that I would not be hindered by my DynCorp record but rather by my lack of an advanced degree and because I did not speak the language of the country in which I was currently residing.

"*Ik ben proberen te spreek het Nederlands, maar het is heel moeilijk,*" I replied in my best Dutch accent.

Elkington paused. I saw Karen shrug at Stephanie.

"Could you please answer in English," Elkington said.

"I said, 'I am trying to speak Dutch, but it is very difficult.'"

Mrs. Hackforth gave a little chuckle.

Elkington then presented the incorrect dates for when I returned from Vienna and showed up for work. I quickly presented the signed letter from my station commander indicating that my absence was beyond my control and that I had reported for duty, along with the Bosnian stamp in my passport, showing precisely what day I returned. So long as I was in Bosnia, I was in the mission territory and entitled, at the very least, to my daily MSA.

By this point, about half an hour into my testimony, I had a good feeling about the tribunal members—and, the best part, they were allowed to question the witnesses directly. It also was not solely up to the barristers to make objections. Chairman Twiss occasionally beat Stephanie to it, stopping Elkington in the midst of badgering me. "We have understood the witness," or "The witness has answered that question numerous times," Twiss would say, looking down over the top of his glasses. "If further clarification is necessary we will seek that from the witness." Elkington would then lean back in his chair (they only stood for opening and closing arguments), looking embarrassed and fumbling through his notes. I sat there, anticipating his questions, knowing I had solid responses that would completely discredit whatever they thought they could make people believe about me.

———

Late in the afternoon, we adjourned for the day, and Jan and I went back to our hotel down the street. We shared a quiet dinner, too exhausted, both emotionally and physically, to say much, then went to bed early. The next morning I woke raring to go.

Next up was Jamie Popwell, the contingent commander. This mission had been his second; previously he had trained civilian police on military and sniper tactics. He was now preparing for his third mission, this time in Kosovo. As far as my team was concerned, Popwell's moment in the spotlight had taken place that day in April 2001 in front of the elevator.

"One day's inaccuracy on a time sheet would be sufficient for dismissal for gross misconduct," he told the tribunal.[4]

"What about a negligent entry?" Stephanie asked. "Would that be gross misconduct?"

"No."

Jan had to contain himself from bursting out in laughter when Popwell answered what he felt his most important daily job function was. Popwell—the contingent commander, in charge of the welfare of DynCorp monitors on the mission—stated, in all seriousness: "Filling out my time sheet."

He admitted that my email had played some part in my redeployment but said the decision had not been his.

"Was the redeployment regarded as a demotion?" Stephanie asked.

"Many people would regard the redeployment as a step down," he admitted.

Several times throughout the day, as Stephanie hammered a point home, usually about the shameful way I had been treated, Chairman Twiss carefully looked down his nose at her. "Let me remind you that we do pick up on things the first time they come across," he would say. Stephanie would beg the pardon of the tribunal, breathe an innocent sigh, twist her hair a little, and appear surprised that the chairman felt she was overdramatizing.

Toward the end of the second day of testimony, Stephanie and Karen told me they had received word from Madeleine: Her immunity had been granted. Now she would be able to testify. Rather than continue to wait for the UN, Madeleine had gone directly to the High Commissioner for Human Rights, who approved the waiver. However, she was now waiting for the official paperwork. After Stephanie presented this news to the panel, the tribunal— overriding DynCorp's objections—was scheduled to reconvene in two months so that Madeleine could testify.[5] Stiers would also be called to testify at that time.

The tribunal was adjourned on April 23, and we packed up my khaki bag, Internet printouts, and all documentation, in anticipation of the hearing in June.

20

VERDICT
(June 2002–May 2003)

We reconvened two months later, on June 25, 2002, with the same tribunal panel: Twiss, Hackworth, and Heckford. Now at the DynCorp table was former Deputy Commissioner J. Michael Stiers, who had done everything in his power to see that I was discredited. But I had Madeleine, one of the seniormost people in the UN mission in Bosnia, by my side.

Stephanie began with her cross-examination of Stiers. He described the meeting on the day after my email as "friendly" and that he had concluded that my email was a "cry for help."

Yes, it was. I did need help—professionally, not personally.

"I told the Applicant that her position was on the line and that she might not come back to her present job," he said.

"So you admit you told the Applicant, 'When you return you won't have your job'?" Stephanie clarified, quoting my statement.

"Yes," Stiers admitted, "but I meant she might have a different job. I was saving the Applicant's neck. I'd been under great pressure to get rid of the Applicant. DynCorp did not want to have any problem with U.S. Monitors and wanted me to ensure that effective action was taken."

"So you had the Applicant demoted?" Stephanie asked.

"No," Stiers insisted, "the redeployment was not a demotion."

Stephanie pushed the point that I, as well as Stiers's own people, Jamie Popwell and Pascal Budge, regarded the redeployment as a demotion, but Stiers held firm, insisting that the change of post was not a demotion but had been for my own good.

Stephanie then presented the evidence I had found: Before heading to Bosnia, when he was the deputy chief of police in Aurora, Colorado, he was sued by a female officer, Barbara Wimmer, who claimed that Stiers and the chief of police had forced her to work in the same office as a coworker who had allegedly stalked, burglarized, beaten, and raped her (and had merely received a written reprimand from the Aurora Police Department). Although Wimmer had applied numerous times for a station transfer, she was told by Stiers: "Get over it and stop running."[1] While Stiers was serving as deputy commissioner in Bosnia, a Colorado jury found both the chief and Stiers guilty of outrageous conduct and each liable for $250,000 of a million-dollar verdict for Wimmer.[2]

As Stephanie read news articles pertaining to Stiers's trial into the record, he went from pale to bright red. He vehemently denied many aspects that had been reported in the press. Although Elkington, the barrister for DynCorp, objected that this information was unrelated to the case at hand, Stephanie countered that it spoke to Stiers's character. Elkington then directed a stinging glare at me, as if I were causing trouble by digging this information up. He demanded to know where I had found the articles.

"The Internet," I said. "And knowing how to do a background investigation, it is all public record and I am, after all, a trained investigator."

But it did not end solely with the charges against Stiers. His successor on the mission, Dennis LaDucer—missing from the proceedings despite the fact that emails to and from him had been entered into the record—had a background that was uncannily similar to Stiers's. I had found that LaDucer had been fired from his assistant sheriff's position in Orange County, California, after five female coworkers filed sexual harassment suits against him. When settlements were finally reached, they topped over $1 million for the plaintiffs (with the county—taxpayer money—covering hundreds of thousands of dollars).[3] Barely a year later, LaDucer was representing the UN mission in Bosnia by speaking at graduation ceremonies of local police officers and by overseeing monitors, such as myself, who were policing crimes against women.

These were my bosses, but more than that, these were the men who held the highest office of authority in the U.S. International Police. They created a boys-will-be-boys environment and turned a blind eye to what, by all accounts, is illegal behavior.

————

Madeleine began her testimony that same day by giving an overview of how the complex system of the UN and related organizations within the mission and the different governing bodies with their various responsibilities under the Dayton Peace Agreement worked together in Bosnia. She was, as usual, very articulate and extremely direct, answering questions in no uncertain terms.

In talking about the creation of the position of gender monitor, which I had held at UN Headquarters, Madeleine said: "This individual was supposed to take the initiative on all aspects of policing which related to gender based violence and this included trafficking. Clearly, this was a totally impossible task."

She described how we met through a referral from Medica Zenica and Main HQ:

Kathy had been recommended very highly, as someone who was very effective, who could actually get the local police to pay attention to gender issues in particular and to the rule of law more generally.... I was very impressed by her commitment, understanding of the issue she had to address, her direct approach and her absolute integrity. She worked very long hours and had far more work than was reasonable. Many of us felt this to be a serious management issue since there were, and indeed are, many in IPTF who have little or nothing to engage them and yet whenever requests were made to find support for Kathy, they were never acceded to.

[Kathy] faced a great deal of hostility from some of the other IPTF officers, particularly the Americans. It was clear that they did not take the issue seriously, almost always referring to the trafficked women as "whores seeking a free ride home." I know of these opinions firsthand since this was also the attitude of those in very senior positions. It was quite clear that lip service was being paid to the need to deal with the issue but that there was no support for doing so in any real sense. This was particularly so in relation to the use of brothels by those in IPTF. Whilst Kathy was being given evidence of the use and abuse that certain IPTF officers were engaged in, there was a complete refusal to accept this at senior levels. Hence there were no real investigations and no one was disciplined. An examination of the records on repatriation will indicate that, although some individuals were returned because of their involvement in using women who had been trafficked... those who were sent home had nothing on their records which indicated the real reasons for their repatriation. It was also apparent that there were no serious investigations into the issue.

Whilst it was clear to the human rights office and the [Office of the High Commissioner on Human Rights] that the work Kathy was doing was of fundamental importance, the opposite opinion was held by many officers.... I cannot help but comment that there seemed to be real concern that she was being too effective and that was inhibiting their freedom.[4]

Madeleine noted that after I was removed from the human rights position, much of the work on trafficking issues came to a halt for several months, crippling the efforts of the Gender Office. She then stunned the room—including the DynCorp legal team—when she disclosed that Deputy Commissioner Dennis LaDucer had himself been caught visiting one of the most notorious brothels in Bosnia.[5] Prior to being repatriated, UN officials asked LaDucer to sign a document, which Madeleine personally saw, indicating that he would be ineligible to work for the UN in any future missions. It was unknown, however, if this document could prevent LaDucer from pursuing another role with DynCorp or any other contractor—would a future employer even know that this UN document existed? *They will now*, I thought, as I turned to look back at the reporters, who were furiously scribbling away.

Prior to the hearing, Stephanie and Karen had requested that DynCorp provide details of all disciplinary actions taken since 1996. In response, DynCorp said the company had identified thirty-eight cases of misconduct, ranging from criminal to administrative, such as assault, alcohol related, prostitution and trafficking, and several violations of UN procedures (abandonment of post, leave abuse, etc.). DynCorp claimed that "most have been terminated for cause"; however, the company cited only nineteen cases as having been terminated for cause—half is not most.

Further, DynCorp was asked to provide details regarding staff members terminated for cause since 1999. Only nine names were cited, one of which was mine (accompanied by the lengthiest description, I might add). One case cited a monitor admitting to using services at a brothel; however, the reason given for sending him home was his participation in the unauthorized Prijedor raid, where the IPTF acted without Policija assistance. But according to SRSG Jacques Klein's press statement, there were *three* American monitors who sent home in regard to the Prijedor raid. Why were the other two not on record? Then there was the case of the station commander, and the stated reason for his termination was that he "admitted to purchasing a female in Sarajevo for 6,000 Deutsch Marks (around $4,000); the female lived with him for several months and then left, allegedly because of a disagreement between the two of them."

Glaringly omitted from the documentation provided by DynCorp was the case of Deputy Commissioner Dennis LaDucer. He was no longer on the mission, and one might think that the outcome of a mission head caught at a brothel known to be involved in the trafficking of women would be—at the very least—termination for cause. It seemed that someone at DynCorp had assumed that we would not have heard about LaDucer, and that this omission would not come back to haunt the company.

LaDucer's picture, like a mug shot, appeared in *The Times* of London, with the caption: "Implicated: Dennis Laducer, a UN Official."[6] The headline revealed all: "Woman sacked for revealing UN links with sex trade."

———

A little over a month later, the tribunal announced its unanimous decision on August 2, 2002. It stated:

> We are driven inexorably to the conclusion that Mr. Stiers, as from 9 October 2000, for whatever reason, had his knife in the Applicant and was determined that she should be removed from her role as a Gender Monitor with IPTF....Mr. Stiers was, we find, an unreliable witness. Not only does his evidence conflict with that of his more junior colleagues but even on its own terms, we find it unpersuasive...[Stiers] said that he redeployed the Applicant for her own good because he thought she was burnt out. Had he sincerely held that belief, we are in no doubt that he would have arranged for a

medical examination of the Applicant at the very least and taken steps to protect her physical and mental health. He took no such steps at all…the Applicant was a marked woman and that officials of IPTF (many of whom were employees of the Respondents) knew that senior officers of IPTF wanted her out.[7]

Karen telephoned me in the apartment I shared with Jan with the news that I had won. There was no mention of a financial settlement yet; in two months we would return to Southampton for the standard remedies hearing, where both sides would once again appear before the panel as its members determined what basic and compensatory damages I was entitled to. Jan and I quietly celebrated—I alternated between crying and laughing. I called my family and was flooded with requests for comments and interviews from the press. Karen prepared an official press statement, and I hoped the larger victory would be that the U.S. State Department would take notice and make long-overdue changes in regard to DynCorp's handling of trafficking issues.

The next morning I called Ben Johnston's attorney in Texas, Kevin Glasheen, to tell him I had won and to firm up the time for my deposition for his case. Glasheen told me DynCorp had contacted him the previous night—only hours after my verdict—with an offer to settle out of court. Johnston had taken the offer, and Glasheen could not give me any more details because the parties had agreed to a gag order. He alluded to the fact that the offer was several times Johnston's salary, and I calculated that it was likely $500,000 or more. I did not blame Johnston for settling, but I was disappointed that no one was going to go after DynCorp in the United States.

———

In September 2002, I was asked to be the opening speaker at the Human Dimension Implementation Meeting's "Anti-Trafficking

Day," a conference in Warsaw, Poland, held by the Organization for
Security and Cooperation in Europe (OSCE) Office for Democratic
Institutions. Members from all UN states would be in attendance. I
prepared a speech outlining the issues I had faced in Bosnia as well
as details from my trial. I was not afraid to make some hard-hitting
points, and wanted to do more than just preach to the choir.

One area that I had noticed needing more attention was training:
training in the field of how to investigate trafficking offenses, not just
training on what trafficking is. In my speech, I explained that if the
OSCE and the UN continued to use contractors to hire and recruit
people for these types of positions, there will be no continuity in the
training process. These positions should be filled by competent individuals who have a long-term desire for project success and completion. Filling one-year contracts with contractors and recruits with
no experience in these matters is negligent and will only result in
complete institutional failure of any legitimate effort. In July 2001,
U.S. Senator Sam Brownback of Kansas, a strong supporter of anti-
trafficking legislation, had told reporters: "International sex trafficking is the new slavery. It includes the classic and awful elements
associated with historic slavery, such as abduction from family and
home, use of false promises, transport to a strange country, loss of
freedom and personal dignity, extreme abuse and depravation." In
addition, he stated that "the biggest problem we face is to convince
people that this is actually taking place."[8]

I proposed that an intense effort be spent on doing just that: con-
vincing people that the problem is real; providing training at all
levels of authority; and holding people accountable, including pushing for the creation of citizens' advisory boards to evaluate all internal affairs complaints, to make recommendations, and to promote
transparent and reliable controls.

I was met with huge applause at the end of my speech and received
offers for further speaking and training engagements. I was also

approached by the delegate from the Holy See, the sovereign entity of the Vatican government, and the only priest in the audience. He thanked me for speaking out on this important issue and praised me and my work. Being raised a Catholic, I felt honored.

————

In the second week of October 2002, the remedies hearing brought Stiers, Budge, and Elkington, whom Jan had nicknamed the "Dalton Gang," along with me and my legal team back to the tribunal. On our first trip to the United States to meet my parents, Jan and I had driven through the Kansas stomping grounds of a group of out-laws called the Dalton Brothers, imagining the days when bad guys were brought to justice with a trusty six-shooter or double-barreled shotgun. Now Chairman Twiss would have to play the role of the hanging judge, Roy Bean. I read the following statement, a version of my opening statement for the first hearing. In it I gave extra emphasis to the difficultly I was having securing employment since my termination:

> These opportunities were all taken from me when DynCorp ter-minated me for cause. It made me ineligible to work in other mis-sions as an American, because DynCorp does all of the recruiting. It also put a severe shadow over my work in Bosnia which would have to be scrutinized by any future or potential employer.
>
> It should be noted that all of the men involved in my demotion and termination have made a career out of being mission contrac-tors and most are still working for DynCorp in some capacity. I have been unable to return to international law enforcement in any capacity, even though many organizations are using my case and experiences as an example and model, and I get continual requests to partake in speaking engagements, seminars and dis-cussions with the press and journalists. All of this is usually in a

quest for advice on how to improve mission policing and human rights investigations. It appears I am still considered somewhat of a liability in regard to my actions when it comes to putting me on the payroll.[9]

I then presented lists of the dozens of jobs I had applied for over the past year without success. I had also secured a witness statement from former IPTF Commissioner Richard Monk, who had been a high-ranking U.K. police officer for 35 years, and who declared that so long as negative accusations were recorded against me, "any future hope of gaining employment within law enforcement work is unrealistic. It is also a fact that within the police fraternity, the fact of her successful appeal against dismissal will not immediately and completely remove the suspicion in some people's mind that some proportion of blame continues to attach to her character."[10]

DynCorp barrister Elkington argued that I could have sought another position with DynCorp. We countered with the evidence that my letter of dismissal stated: "You will no longer be eligible for employment consideration in the future with DynCorp." But even better was Mrs. Hackforth's response to Elkington: "Did you honestly believe that Ms. Bolkovac should have applied to a position within this company?"

After hours of defending damages for injury to feelings, distress, and humiliation (the tribunal's terms), I broke down and began to cry. Chairman Twiss asked if I would like to testify in private chambers, but I refused. I wanted the press and DynCorp to know what I had gone through. I stared right at Budge and pointed at him. "I had to explain to my fellow law enforcement officers and to my own children that I had been fired after being accused of falsifying time sheets and gross misconduct. I know you have children, Pascal. How would you feel telling your children that?"

Again the findings regarding compensation would not be rendered for some weeks and would be sent via mail. As we awaited the determination, DynCorp filed an appeal, asserting that the tribunal had not properly interpreted previous cases cited in its decision. DynCorp had settled with Johnston in the United States but was appealing my case? I could not understand why DynCorp would want to drag this out further.

Regardless of the appeal, the remedies decision was delivered on November 22, 2002. Again the tribunal ruled unanimously. "It is hard to imagine a case in which a firm has acted in a more callous, spiteful and vindictive manner towards a former employee," Mr. Twiss said in his remarks. Although the damages for compensation of lost earnings due to unfair dismissal and for, as the decision stated, "injury to feelings" were an inordinately high sum for a UK tribunal, they amounted only to around $175,000. One third of the sum went to cover my legal fees and at least $35,000 had been expended the previous year prior to the trial to cover my living expenses, travel to attorney meetings, child support and college expenses for two of my three children. What I was left with was not a huge sum of money, but my pride was intact and my faith in the justice system was renewed. Besides, unlike Ben Johnston, I was free to talk, and to keep talking, about what had happened. And to write.

I would not see a penny until after the appeal hearing, which meant I would have to wait another six months for our scheduled date of May 2, 2003. As the time passed, my team and DynCorp exchanged the required paperwork and statements.

Two days before the appeal hearing was to take place, Elkington contacted my legal team and dropped the case. I finally received my damages, with interest.

ZERO TOLERANCE
(May 2003–2010)

Three days after dropping the appeal, DynCorp issued a press release that the U.S. State Department had awarded it a $22 million contract to police Iraq. DynCorp used my case to announce to the world that it had adopted a "new corporate culture" and that ethical indiscretions would not happen again. As the *Chicago Tribune* reported: "A senior State Department official, Paul Kelly, assured U.S. Rep. Henry Hyde (R-Ill.) this week that his department has been working with DynCorp to prevent a repetition of the revelations by Kathryn Bolkovac, a former Omaha [*sic*] police officer hired by DynCorp for a UN-administered International Police Task Force that played the same advisory role in Bosnia now being envisioned for Iraq."[1]

So now I was the DynCorp poster girl.

I had served on the U.S. government's first rent-a-cop experiment. Despite clear warning signs, the State Department had deemed the international police mission in Bosnia a success and worthy of replication. Virtually overnight, DynCorp—along with its competitors and their conveniently opaque subsidiaries, spin-offs, and rebrands such as Halliburton, Brown & Root, Blackwater/XE, and Titan—became billion-dollar companies as well as powerful political machines. Over the years DynCorp would go on to win more government contracts. In Iraq alone, its contract was renewed in 2007 for another two years—despite a tarnished record there,[2] in which DynCorp could not properly account for most of the $1.2 billion it received from the US State Department to train Iraqi police.[3]

Not only was DynCorp flush with cash but, unlike the military, it was full of willing bodies. Why? My answer: DynCorp welcomed with open arms recruits with insufficient training and questionable motives who eagerly enrolled in its high-paying, zero-accountability, travel-abroad programs. Sure there were legal mishaps, killings here and there, drug and weapons smuggling, some rapes caught on videotape, and major accounting blunders, but none of this seemed to get in the way of DynCorp operations. For DynCorp, government contracts were practically on auto-renew. Taxpayer money kept pouring in as more and more contractors were shipped out around the world: Haiti, Kosovo, Liberia, Serbia, East Timor, Iraq, Afghanistan, the list goes on.

———

Of course, it is entirely possible that over the years my case actually effected some positive change—that the claims of greater efforts, zero tolerance, and education had indeed influenced the way these missions operated. Unfortunately, however, according to what I was hearing, the story on the ground was not the same as the one in the glossy brochure. I was repeatedly contacted by DynCorp employees who had been wrongfully terminated and who had witnessed serious infractions.

In July 2009 I returned a call from a man who had left a mysterious message for me saying it was regarding DynCorp. I was reluctant to return his call right away, as I was not comfortable with the way he had tracked me down through a previous employer, who had alerted me. A few weeks later, however, I did call the number he had left. After I confirmed that I was, indeed, Kathy of *Bolkovac v. DynCorp,* he exhaled in relief and thanked me for calling him back. He spouted bits and parts of a story that was all too familiar: A good friend of his, a former cop from Albuquerque, New Mexico, had signed a contract with DynCorp and was now in protective custody in Kabul after blowing the whistle on what he termed "immoral behavior by the top brass." The caller alleged abuse of a local Afghani boy, telling me that "DynCorp's whitewashing the story" by saying a boy was asked to perform a ritual dance for a DynCorp party. It was way more than that, he insisted. "And there's a videotape." He also stated that his friend was "scared to death of DynCorp." Later that month the *Washington Post* would break the story, stating: "DynCorp fired four senior managers in Afghanistan over the party and other incidents, according to employees who spoke on the condition of anonymity because they feared retaliation."[4] What, I wondered, were these "other incidents"?

In the fall of 2009 I received an email from a young woman who had been on the Iraq contract with DynCorp and was now on a second DynCorp contract in Sudan. She had made an email complaint to a DynCorp "anonymous" hotline about her supervisor, whom she claimed had been on paid vacation leave for seventy-six days and who was not there to address a discrepancy in her pay schedule that left her underpaid by $10,000. Her supposedly anonymous complaint ended up in the hands of said supervisor. Soon after she was fired for "falsifying her time sheets"—a line I was quite familiar with. In a phone conversation, she told me she had to buy her own airline ticket home and was served a notice that she was also responsible for reimbursing DynCorp for flying her to Sudan at the start of the mission. When she appealed this decision, her supervisor retorted: "You don't know who you're messing with."

In order to satisfy my own curiosity, I asked her if she recognized any of the names of the gentlemen who testified at my trial. Popwell's name was familiar: He was the DynCorp program manager in Sudan. I shook my head in disbelief but was not surprised. I gave her the name of my attorneys in the United Kingdom, only to discover that there had indeed been one very big change since my lawsuit: DynCorp—now the U.S. State Department's largest contractor—had moved its legal jurisdiction to Dubai, one of the United Arab Emirate states. This would make it virtually impossible for new lawsuits to be tried expeditiously and effectively.

Likewise, news was circulating that DynCorp's major competitors, such as Halliburton/KBR, proactively tailored their contracts to include clauses blocking employees from the right to sue the company—even in cases of serious crimes, such as rape and assault. This was the impetus for U.S. Senator Al Franken's 2009 bill, Senate Amendment 2588, which prohibits federal contracts with companies that force their employees to sign such above-the-law clauses.[5]

Madeleine Rees, after over a decade of tireless and driven service, was removed from her post by the UN when her contract was not renewed. Unafraid of conflict, Madeleine had been the thorn in the UN's side over my case and many similar incidents involving immoral and illegal activities. Because of pending litigation, Madeleine was not able to go into detail, but summarized things to me as: "more of the same."

———

Despite DynCorp's expanding dossier of firing whistleblowers, the men who testified against me—and who were ruled to be not credible and of having acted in discriminatory, malicious ways—were not fired or even demoted. They kept their high-level positions. Several, such as Pascal Budge and Jamie Popwell, have since been promoted to the high-level management positions within DynCorp.

Given this chain of command, what is the likelihood of achieving significant and widespread improvement?

DynCorp is a company that likes to keep a low profile. In its view, the less the general public is aware of it, the better. In my view, even a two-year-old knows it is much easier to get away with bad behavior when no one is looking. In the years I worked for DynCorp, I became privy to some amazing taxpayer abuse: sketchy billing, overstaffing, puffed-up budgets, half-finished or barely touched projects, shoddily trained staff, and a prevailing attitude of "DynCorp isn't worrying about it, why should you?" It was well known that our checks would keep coming regardless of overall job performance. But this just scrapes the surface.

It would be easy to attribute the misbehavior to isolated incidents by a couple of bad apples, as DynCorp, the State Department, and factions of the UN would like people to believe. But the disappearance of files from human trafficking cases that implicated DynCorp personnel, the abrupt and unexplained cancellation of legitimate human rights investigations, men from around the globe getting away with buying and raping teenage girls—these are not isolated incidents and cannot be dismissed as merely the actions of a few rogue individuals.

I recognize that, like any random group of individuals, all police forces can have some bad apples; and I can't deny that some cops still subscribe to the unwritten code that they should cover for their fellow officers, or at least turn a blind eye to misconduct. But that is not how Hawk trained me. Police officers should be held to a higher standard, both morally and legally.

It was ordinary conscience that compelled me to blow the whistle on DynCorp. I was the first American police officer to go public with these allegations, and it did not occur to me to dwell on the fact that I was going up against one of the largest and most powerful corporations in the world or that the outcome would be exactly what one might expect from a billion-dollar company fighting an individual: The company would survive and thrive.

———

I have spent many sleepless nights over the past several years wondering why these blatantly illegal behaviors were simply allowed to be swept under the rug. And yet reports of immoral and illegal behavior among DynCorp's civilian peacekeepers worldwide—as well as by members of UN peacekeeping missions in general—continue to make front-page news with alarming regularity.

Allegations of sexual assault and human rights violations by UN peacekeepers have been brought forth on missions in the Congo, Sierra Leone, Burundi, Guinea, Nigeria, Liberia, Bosnia, Kosovo, Haiti, Cambodia, Colombia, Sudan, Iraq, and Afghanistan. A huge percentage have involved DynCorp, causing Amnesty International in 2003 to declare DynCorp "a private company with a dubious policing record."[6]

For example, in 2007 the Permanent People's Tribunal, an international gathering of state heads, law experts, and activists to expose human rights abuses, held a hearing entitled "Accusation Against the Transnational DynCorp," in which it compiled a nearly sixty-page report citing DynCorp for offenses against humanity, including DynCorp contractors' alleged involvement in drug trafficking (which resulted in the deaths of two DynCorp employees) and a videotape of DynCorp contractors sexually violating underage Colombian girls. The video had been reproduced and sold in the main streets of Bogotá. After learning of the tape, one of the victims shown in the footage committed suicide. No official investigation against the men on tape has ever taken place—they simply returned to the United States without fear of any legal action or record against them. During the tribunal, the Colombian Commission on Human Rights took fundamental issue with organizations' use of mercenaries for profit during settings of war, conflict, and political instability, stating:

> Former members of police or military forces, working for agencies like DynCorp, do not only strip themselves of their uniform, but also of their oaths and honor, which they had assumed to guarantee the security of their respective Nation-States and to safeguard the interests of their community. Once they entered into the logic of being mercenaries, these subjects divested themselves of any responsibility or social loyalty and became the potential victimizers of any community in the world.[7]

In April 2008 a Senate Democratic Policy Committee Hearing entitled "Contracting Abuses in Iraq: Is the Bush Administration Safeguarding American Taxpayer Dollars?" took place on Capitol Hill. Three former military contractors from Halliburton, Kellogg Brown and Root (KBR), and a subcontractor of DynCorp testified to abuse of local Iraqis, such as denying Iraqi employees clean water; graft and gouging, such as billing the government for projects that never were completed or never even begun and double-billing for laptop computers, food, and vehicles; the black-market procurement of weapons; and contractor involvement in a prostitution ring. According to testimony by Barry Halley, a technology consultant and former Marine employed by a DynCorp subcontractor in Iraq:

> A co-worker was killed when he was traveling in an unsecure car and shot performing a high-risk mission. I believe that my co-worker could have survived if he had been riding in an armored car. At the time, the armored car that he would otherwise have been riding in was being used by a manager to transport prostitutes from Kuwait to Baghdad. Although the activities had been going on for some

time, nothing was done to stop it. Eventually, the ringleader was pulled from his managerial position. But he wasn't fired. Rather, he was transferred to another post on a contract in Haiti.[8]

On and on it goes. On September 1, 2009, a watchdog group, the Project on Government Oversight, sent a plea to U.S. Secretary of State Hillary Clinton after six contractors stationed in Kabul, through the firm Wackenhut, filed individual complaints on what has been described as a *Lord of the Flies* environment, with supervisors routinely victimizing UN workers, contractors, and Afghan nationals, including urinating on them and forcing them to drink alcohol, which is against religious and state law. Videos and photos showed scenes of blindfolded, drunk, and nude guards—hired to guard the U.S. Embassy—as well as women believed to be prostitutes. The whistleblowers described how these frequent parties were used as intimidation tactics and hazing rituals, forced on unwilling participants. An embassy official stated that the nearly 100 percent annual turnover rate in guards on that mission attests to the lack of mutual respect, group cohesion, and professionalism and had severely threatened the safety of thousands of employees at the U.S. Embassy who rely on them for protection in one of the most dangerous regions in the world.[9] News of these guards gone wild was even featured on late-night talk show *Jimmy Kimmel Live* with a segment, "Cabo or Kabul?" The audience had to guess if a photo was of spring break in Cabo San Lucas or of security guards in Kabul. The audience got each picture wrong—all the photos were from Kabul.

I can only imagine what these missions are hiding that has not yet or will never make the news. But none of these stories answers the question of why the outrageous conduct continues rather than leading to concerted efforts to change bad practices. There is no box that recruits have to check if they committed a felony on a previous mission, for there is no such thing as a felony when you have immunity.

To quote Human Rights Report author Martina Vandenberg, from her testimony "Legal Options to Stop Human Trafficking" before a Senate Judiciary Subcommittee in 2007: "With zero prosecutions, zero tolerance has zero credibility."[10]

———

Although a system of contractors for hire might seem reasonable to supplement and support U.S. military presence in wartorn regions, the outcome has been the creation of a band of mercenaries—a secretive, unregulated, well-paid, under-the-radar force that is larger than the U.S. Army. Worse, the framework for recruiting, enticing, and managing this band is severely and dangerously flawed. After DynCorp had been in Iraq for nearly four years, in 2008 the State Department Inspector General for Iraq Reconstruction, Stuart Bowen, wrote in an audit that the State Department "does not know specifically what it received for most of the $1.2 billion in expenditures" under its DynCorp contract.[11]

In the United States, police work is a highly regulated profession; officers at all levels, from city to federal, are held to clear standard operating procedures, moral and ethical codes of conduct, and the highest levels of accountability. Our government should not take worldwide policing so lightly that it is simply passed off to the lowest bidder.

That is not to say that advances haven't occurred. The 2007 Defense Bill extended the reach of the Military Extraterritorial Jurisdiction Act (MEJA) to cover not just the military overseas but to also place contractors accompanying the military and working in a war zone under the Uniform Code of Military Justice (UCMJ). As Peter W. Singer of the Brookings Institute described the new law, "Basically 100,000 contractors woke up to find themselves potentially under the same set of military laws that govern the armed forces....It's the single biggest legal development for the private military industry since its start." Still, Singer was skeptical. "It holds the potential, and I emphasize 'potential' here, to finally bring some legal status and accountability to a business that has expanded well past the laws."[12]

And yet there were still loopholes—it was not clear exactly how UCMJ applied to private contractors who were not accompanying military, as in my case, contracted through the Department of State, not the Department of Defense.

In February 2010, Senator Patrick Leahy (D-VT) and Congressman David Price (D-NC) introduced companion bills that would close this gap through the Civilian Extraterritorial Jurisdiction Act (CEJA), which would hold all American government employees and contractors working overseas accountable to U.S. Law. CEJA proposes that the Justice Department set up means to investigate alleged abuses, that federal agents be authorized to arrest alleged offenders outside the United States if there is probable cause, and that the Attorney General be required to provide annual reports to Congress on the number of offenses filed, investigated, and prosecuted, and, importantly, whether any changes are needed in the law to make it more effective.

Only time will tell if this new law will make a difference.

I recommend these policies for all police officers recruited for international missions:

- Minimum of eight to ten years experience
- Thorough background checks by federal agencies, not haphazard telephone interviews and mailed-in recommendations
- Intensive training programs conducted by veteran international police, not led by corporate managers or ex-Army officers with no expertise in international law or police investigations
- A clear understanding that police work is not about making money; it is about a calling to serve justice at all levels

These are crucial steps, but the only way I see to truly change the system is by not allowing our government to outsource any civilian police operations. The government needs to take steps to create a force of civilian police—as exists in most European countries—that would also serve abroad as needed. The force would not necessarily be a national police force, but its members must maintain ties and accountability to their home police departments through extended leaves of absence to serve abroad. This method would allow the officers to maintain seniority, benefits, and retirement as an incentive for the time in a mission. A civilian government authority must take responsibility for these police officers, not a private corporation. In this way, citizens of the United States of America will be directly representing the morals and values of their nation rather than outsourcing them.

Whatever the reasons we are fighting wars overseas, regardless of whether we agree with them ideologically, we should not lose sight of the greater mission at hand. And we should not be doing greater harm.

NOTES

Chapter 4: Sarajevo

1. Adam B. Siegel, "Civil-Military Marriage Counseling: Can This Union Be Saved?" *The Journal of Humanitarian Assistance* (2002): 30.

Chapter 5: "Accidents" Happen

1. John F. Burns, "Racing through Snipers' Alley on Ride to Sarajevo," *New York Times*, September 26, 1992.
2. UK Employment Tribunal, *Bolkovac v. DynCorp*, case number 3102729/01, Reserved Decision, July 1, 2002.
3. Human Rights Case# 99/ILI/267, Ilidza region, 1999.
4. International Crisis Group, "Policing the Police in Bosnia: A Further Reform Agenda," May 10, 2002, 7.
5. UK Employment Tribunal, *Bolkovac v. DynCorp*, case number 3102729/01, Reserved Decision, July 1, 2002.

Chapter 7: At the Florida

1. John McGhie, "Women for Sale," BBC News, broadcast on June 8, 2000.

Chapter 8: The Gender Desk

1. www.un.org, Press Release SG/A/848.

Chapter 9: No Incidents

1. Human Rights Case #00-TUZ-094, Tuzla region, 2000.
2. P. W. Singer, *Corporate Warriors: The Rise of the Privatized Military Industry* (New York: Cornell University Press, 2007), 140.

Chapter 10: Education of a Lifetime

1. Alix Kroeger, "Sarajevo's Tunnel of Hope," BBC News, April 16, 2001.

Chapter 11: Ladies of the Evening

1. Human Rights Case #00-ORA-150, Doboj region, September 30, 2000.

Chapter 12: "Thinking with Our Hearts"

1. Human Rights Office Brčko, "Trafficking and Prostitution," January 10, 2000.

Chapter 13: Backlash

1. UK Employment Tribunal, *Bolkovac v. DynCorp*, case number 3102729/01, Reserved Decision, July 1, 2002.
2. Ibid.

Chapter 14: The Prijedor Raids

1. Human Rights Watch, "Bosnia and Herzegovina," Vol. 14, No. 9 (D), November 2002, 49.
2. Ibid., 50.
3. Ibid., 57.
4. Colum Lynch, "Misconduct, Corruption by U.S. Police Mar Bosnia Mission," *Washington Post*, May 29, 2001.

Chapter 15: Distaste

1. Scott Parks, "Whistleblower, Fearing Retaliation from Gangsters, Flees Bosnia for Life in Texas," *Dallas Morning News*, March 14, 2001.
2. Human Rights Watch, "Bosnia and Herzegovina," Vol. 14, No. 9 (D), November 2002, 67.
3. Scott Parks, "Whistleblower, Fearing Retaliation from Gangsters, Flees Bosnia for Life in Texas," *Dallas Morning News*, March 14, 2001.
4. Reuters, "Bosnian Club Raids Set 177 Women Free," March 3, 2001.
5. Human Rights Watch, "Bosnia and Herzegovina," Vol. 14, No. 9 (D), November 2002, 59.

Chapter 16: Time Sheets

1. UK Employment Tribunal, *Bolkovac v. DynCorp*, case number 3102729/01, Reserved Decision, July 1, 2002.

2. Colum Lynch, "U.N. Halted Probe of Officers' Alleged Role in Sex Trafficking; Lack of Support from Above, in Field Impeded Investigators," *Washington Post*, December 27, 2001.

Chapter 17: Going to the Press

1. Tanya Domi, "The UN Mission in Bosnia Comes under Fire for Allegedly Trying to Cover up a Prostitution Scandal," *Oslobodenje*, July 20, 2001.

Chapter 18: The Khaki Duffel Bag

1. UNMIBH (United Nations Mission in Bosnia Herzegovina), "Building a Better Future Together, December 1995 to June 2002," www.un.org; STOP International, www.stopinternational.org, biography of de Lavarene.
2. Human Rights Watch, "Bosnia and Herzegovina," Vol. 14, No. 9 (D), November 2002, 185.
3. *Boys Will Be Boys*, BBC documentary, June 16, 2002.
4. Stop International, www.stopinternational.org.
5. *Hardtalk*, BBC, Monday, October 22, 2001.
6. *Boys Will Be Boys*, BBC documentary, June 16, 2002.
7. Scott Parks, "Whistleblower, Fearing Retaliation from Gangsters, Flees Bosnia for Life in Texas," *Dallas Morning News*, March 14, 2001.

Chapter 19: Tribunal

1. UK Employment Tribunal, *Bolkovac v. DynCorp*, case number 3102729/01, Reserved Decision, July 1, 2002.
2. Ibid.
3. Ibid.
4. Ibid.
5. Ibid.

Chapter 20: Verdict

1. Rocky Mountain News, "Federal Jury Awards Former Aurora Police Officer $1 Million," January 20, 2000; interview with Barbara Wimmer, July 13–14, 2010.
2. Ibid.
3. Daniel Yi, "O.C. to Pay $325,000 in 1 of 5 Sex Harassment Suits Against LaDucer," *Los Angeles Times*, March 3, 1999.
4. UK Employment Tribunal, *Bolkovac v. DynCorp*, case number 3102729/01, Reserved Decision, July 1, 2002.
5. Daniel McGrory, "The Seamy Side of Peacekeeping; Whistle-Blower Vindicated After Being Fired for Exposing UN Ties to Prostitution Racket," *The Sunday Herald-Observer*, August 11, 2002.

6. Daniel McGrory, "Implicated: Dennis Laducer, a UN Official," *The Times* (London), August 7, 2002, p. 1B.
7. UK Employment Tribunal, *Bolkovac v. DynCorp*, case number 3102729/01, Reserved Decision, July 1, 2002.
8. Press Release, "Wellstone, Brownback Praise Trafficking Report," July 12, 2001.
9. UK Employment Tribunal, *Bolkovac v. DynCorp*, case number 3102729/01, Reserved Decision, July 1, 2002.
10. Ibid.

Chapter 21: Zero Tolerance

1. John Crewdson, "Contractor Tries to Avert Repeat of Bosnia Woes: Sex Scandal Still Haunts DynCorp," *Chicago Tribune*, May 13, 2002.
2. James Glanz, "U.S. Agency Finds New Waste and Fraud in Iraqi Rebuilding Projects," *New York Times*, February 1, 2007.
3. CNN online, www.cnn.com, "Most of $1.2 billion to train Iraqi police unaccounted for," October 23, 2007.
4. Ellen Nakashima, "Amid Reviews, DynCorp Bolsters Ethics Practices," *Washington Post*, July 27, 2009.
5. Chris McGreal, "Rape case to force US defence firms into the open," *The Guardian* (UK), October 15, 2009.
6. Amnesty International, "A Catalogue of Failures: G8 Arms Exports and Human Rights Violations," May 18, 2003, Section 2.3.1.
7. Permanent People's Tribunal Session on Colombia, "Accusation against the Transnational Dyncorp," February 24–27, 2007.
8. Senate Democratic Policy Committee Hearing, "Contracting Abuses in Iraq: Is the Bush Administration Safeguarding American Taxpayer Dollars?," April 2008.
9. Letter from Project on Government Oversight to Hillary Clinton, September 1, 2009.
10. Prepared Statement of Martina Vandenberg before the Senate Judiciary Subcommittee on Human Rights, "Legal Options to Stop Human Trafficking," March 26, 2007.
11. Statement of Stuart Bowen, Jr., Special Inspector General, U.S. Senate Committee on Appropriations, "The Effectiveness of U.S. Efforts to Combat Corruption, Waste, Fraud and Abuse in Iraq," March 11, 2008.
12. Peter W. Singer, "Frequently Asked Questions on the UCMJ Change and its Applicability to Private Military Contractors," The Brookings Institution, January 12, 2007.

INDEX

INDEX